WHAT OTHERS ARE SAYING

The gateway to a rich, delicious and satisfying second chapter of life awaits you! Brian Lukyn takes a refreshing look at finding deeper meaning and fulfillment on a daily basis and redefines wellness for a generation seeking to live life to the fullest.

Marilena Minucci, MS, CHC, BCC
www.QuantumCoachingMethod.com

The Un-Retirement Guide takes a unique look at the elephant in the room...baby boomers who are unable or unwilling to retire.
Do yourself a favor and make this book part of your required reading and then plan for your un-retirement!

Leslie J. Smith, B.A., LL.B.
Lawyer, Deputy Judge, Mediator, Speaker
Author of best seller "Legal Ease: Essential Legal Strategies to Protect Canadian Non-union Employees"

This wonderful humanoid is adventurous in work, play and writing. He is kind hearted with compassion and curiosity for others, coupled with a hunger for personal growth, wellbeing and health. These words describe a few of the traits of Brian Lukyn I have observed over the past 30 years.

Carol Keane Counsellor, Healer and Friend

Like many baby boomers, Brian faced the need to take a serious look at whether retirement was even feasible or desired at 65 years of age. After much research he has skillfully introduced us to the "Un-Retirement Guide™"; strategies, tools and information to not only survive but thrive in un-retirement. This book is a thought-provoking guide as you address the questions in facing your own retirement. I highly recommend it.

Linda Olson,
CEO of Christian Speakers Get Paid
Amazon #1 Bestseller, "Uncovering the Champion Within."

I like this book, "The Un-Retirement Guide^{TM}," by Brian Lukyn. It is comprehensive and clearly laid out by someone who's been there. The author knows firsthand the challenges and how it feels to be older and facing an uncertain future. You will find this book to evoke hope and give you practical information to successfully un-retire.

Glen E. Klassen
Chartered Accountant
Author of "Evansing, Heart of The Irish Kingdom" and "Unlimited - Anything is Possible"

I know Brian as a serious seeker of truth with a great sense of humor. He can laugh at himself when caught in human foibles; commit himself to any true calling and friend; and venture where only the brave dare go. He is a mentor, teacher and friend to many – often finding heart in the midst of trauma, and sharing his keen wit and insight with those who seek to find their truth and path.
Brian has a fine mind and a gentle heart. I enjoy his presence and trust his instincts and wisdom.

Henri McKinnon, Founding Director of Insight Counselling and Training Inc.

The Un-retirement Guide™ *demonstrates Brian has listened to the individuals he serves and experienced many of their middle age hardships. His message on "un-retirement," is a heartfelt effort to first analyze and then prescribe a readable solution for working up to and beyond the once traditional retirement age. Read it and relax for there is an answer.*

Mike Lukyn Former Teacher

Brian Lukyn brings a wealth of experience, pragmatism, and perseverance to an important area of our culture. Without being pedantic or alarmist, he addresses this poignant topic with humor, caring and clarity. It is obvious he challenges himself and others to get the best out of life.

Kevin Hale International Educator

As a Physiotherapist working in the field of occupational health and ergonomics, I have known and had the pleasure to work with Brian Lukyn for over 15 years. Brian has years of experience and wisdom as a Rehabilitation Counselor in helping others be their best. He is an excellent communicator, who understands cultural diversity and differing values, and is a seasoned advocate for injured workers. Brian practices what he preaches and maintains his inner equilibrium and his personal growth through a wellness lifestyle. I am confident that The Un-Retirement Guide™ *will be an important resource for all of us who juggle our personal or work goals in healthy and sustainable ways.*

Klari Varallyai Physiotherapist, Ergonomic Consultant.
Assistant Clinical Professor School of Physical Therapy
Faculty of Medicine U.B.C.   BC. Canada.

Many of us in middle age talk of needing to make a change in our lives and then do nothing about it. I have watched Brian, with admiration as he has embarked on a journey of re-inventing himself as a writer over the last couple of years. They say to write what you know and it looks like Brian has done just that!

Brian Cebryk Unretired

As an employment specialist and a wellness coach, Brian provides truthful and valuable insight into how to get clear on your desired future and achieve it. This book will guide you in finding your purpose as you transition into your desired retirement.

Lauren McKenzie Teacher of Yoga and Wellness Coach

While working with Brian Lukyn on the "North Island Fisheries Initiative" program in the 1990's, I was able to see first-hand his ability, through his use of humor, personal experiences and empathy, to successfully assist older resource workers through a challenging employment transition. With these attributes Brian's, **"The Un-Retirement Guide™"** *is what the career development community and older workers need to assist them as they navigate through the current labour market shift.*

Paul Curtis, B.Sc., RRP, Employment Coordinator and Advisor

"Un-retirement-what a great word! I am one of those baby boomers that doesn't plan on retiring at the conventional age of 65 and I know I am not alone! Brian's book is very intriguing and full of useful information for myself and fellow boomers! He has addressed an interesting and fashionable topic with great wisdom, clarity and sufficient research. There are an unprecedented number of us coming into "un-retirement years." It is very encouraging to read what Brian has written and know that I can apply some of his ideas and suggestions to my own life. Thank you, Brian.

Margie McIntyre, Financial agent and coach. Author of "Mind Matters - Change Your Mind, Change Your Life!"

When I was first asked years ago, to provide in-house training for Brian in the area of rehabilitation counselling, I thought it might be an uphill climb as he was fairly new to the field, and already in his mid-career. This quickly proved not to be the case. In career and rehabilitation counselling, it is obvious that "old" is often a stereotype and/or personal choice, not a number. When we stop looking for new ideas, when we try to rely on what we already know, so that we can survive the rest of our life, then we have become old. Brian has inspired me to take on challenges I had denied myself for many years, and stay young. Thanks Brian, you trained me well.

Cliff Dundas BA, CCRC, CDMS, RRP, Senior Rehabilitation Counsellor

The Un-Retirement™ guide is informative and well researched. Brian brings a wealth of knowledge given his occupation and personal background. Brian talks about "winning the race sooner rather than later" and expands on how this may have different meanings for all of us. As we start thinking about retirement this is a great tool to reflect and plan for what lies ahead.

Suzanne D. Jubb, Author, "The Golden Goose, One Important Step to Financial Freedom"

I expected this resource to be helpful and good when Brian Lukyn mentioned he was writing it. What I didn't expect was that it would be such a thorough and complete transformation guide for any person who is approaching the all-important life decision, "To retire? Or Not to retire?" It is fully engaging as it guides 50+ Boomers to be equipped to embrace the next season in their life.

Kathleen D. Mailer, International Business Evangelist, #1 Best Selling Author (including "Prepare to Prosper, Taking Your Business To A HIGHER Level"), Founder/Facilitator of "A Book Is Never A Book Boot Camp", Editor-In-Chief of "Today's Businesswoman Magazine".

The Un-Retirement Guide™

A Complete Life Wellness Plan™

for 50+ Boomers Needing to Succeed!

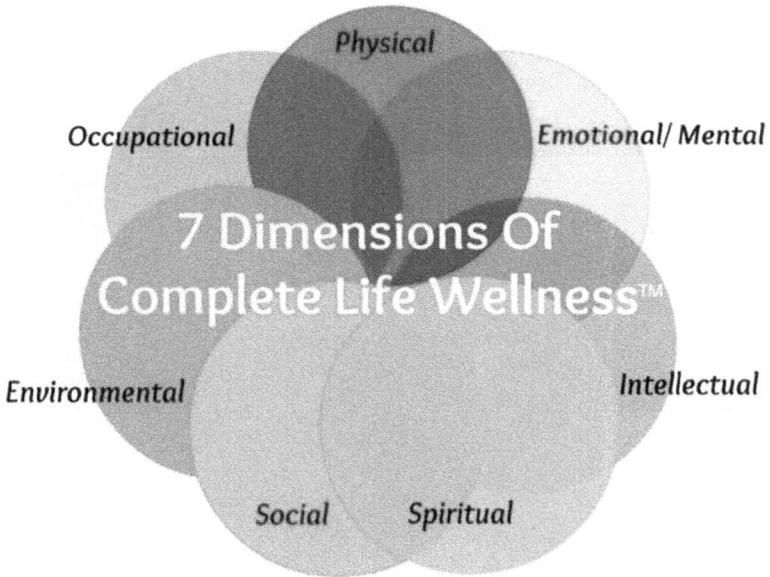

Physical

Occupational

Emotional/ Mental

7 Dimensions Of
Complete Life Wellness™

Environmental

Intellectual

Social   Spiritual

Brian Lukyn

Library of Canada
Lukyn, Brian.
Title: The Un-Retirement Guide™
Sub-Title: *A Complete Life Wellness Plan*^{TM}
for 50+ Boomers Needing to Succeed!
Copyright © 2015 by Brian Lukyn
Lukyn Enterprises
ISBN: 978-0-9948511-0-9

Published by: BrianLukyn.com

DEDICATION

I dedicate this labour of love to the unretired Baby Boomers it was written for.

I include my brother Justin Michael here, who supported me through thick or thin over the decades of our lives, he is also a man who loves books and understands the amount of work that goes into writing one.

My son Beau I add to this list and dedicate this guidebook to, as he is a kindred spirit who relentlessly works towards understanding and expressing his creativity in the world of hand drawn and virtual art.

Finally, I add my friend and long term believer in my potential, Carol. Thanks for being there.

ACKNOWLEDGEMENTS

For my editor Coralie J. Banks, of Leaping Cowgirl Productions for her unwavering guidance and hard work.

To Kathleen Mailer of Aurora Publishing who introduced me to this fascinating and complex world of writing, publishing and marketing.

CONTENTS

INTRODUCTION

Hi there and welcome to the inside of The Un-Retirement Guide™.

I'm so excited you are here on this page with me. I'm going to get right down to things and start by asking a few questions to see if any resonate for you.

- Is there a growing awareness how *critical* the state of your health is to staying employed and your overall quality of life?
- Does the prospect of having to keep working, with no end in sight feel overwhelming?
- Can you afford to retire but enjoy working and want to keep doing so?
- Do you feel like something is missing in your life and aren't sure what?
- In the workplace, are you discriminated against because of your age?
- Are you uncertain of what your job qualifications are, or if you have any transferable skills?
- Are you employed or unemployed and searching for work?

Does any of this grab your attention? **The Un-Retirement Guide™** explores these questions and others that Boomers struggle with.

Beyond this are exercises, tools and strategies to holistically steer your life.

The Un-Retirement Guide™ is structured as follows:

Part 1 Un-Retirement 101

The Un-Retirement Guide™ is not a guide to financial planning like the reams of other books written on this subject. By this point in our lives we're aware of the long term need of having a plan to set money aside, which is often easier said than done. Read on to know more.

This section is therefore brief and focuses on demystifying the concept of retirement and un-retirement. It also defines a term commonly used in relation to financial security known as "standard of living" and includes a simple tool for calculating yours.

Part 2 Investing in your Future

Part 2 explains the nuts and bolts of Health and Wellness, and why it is pivotal to your *work and non-work success*. It also delves into the seven dimensions of wellness and eventual creation of your Complete Life Wellness Plan™.

Part 3 Staying Gainfully Employed and More

Finally, part 3 consists of a 5-chapter series, which addresses our needs in the occupational dimension. This includes a comprehensive look at career management (including how to perform a targeted job search) for the older worker, countering age discrimination, coping with workplace stressors and self-employment. The contents of these chapters are designed to optimize your odds of staying gainfully employed.

Part 1
Un-Retirement 101

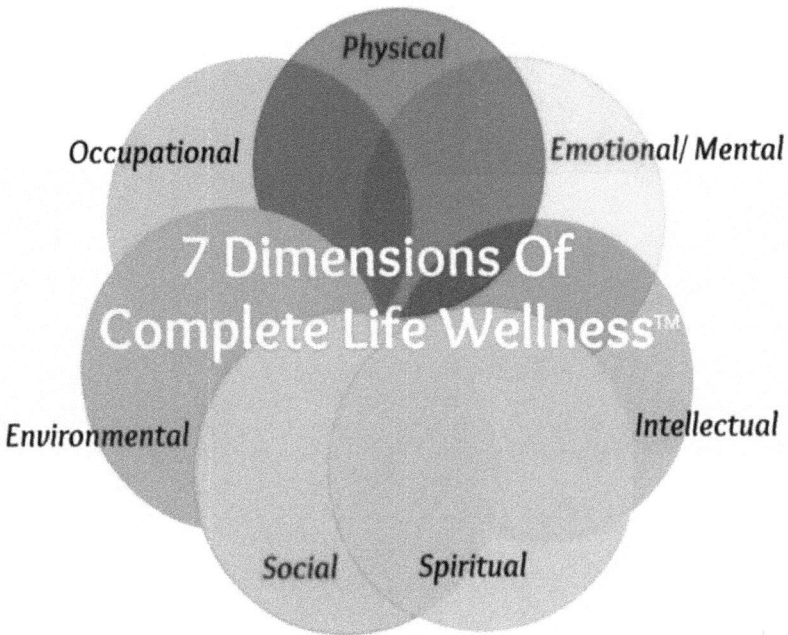

Physical

Occupational

Emotional/ Mental

7 Dimensions Of
Complete Life Wellness™

Environmental

Intellectual

Social   Spiritual

WHEN CAN YOU RETIRE? I CAN'T YET

Chapter One

A man is not old until regrets take the place of dreams.
John Barrymore

It was 2004 by the time my divorce papers were signed off on, ending two years of legal wrangling and a test of my sanity. The costs of settling this matter included money; heartache; loss of momentum and chronic stressors, to name a few.

After the dust had settled, I recall sitting at my favourite nature spot one morning, on the bank of a local river. Watching the fast moving water, and listening to the different sounds it made, helped me relax. There was a fresh, cool breeze that smelled of the forest that travelled with the river en route to the sea. Gradually, a renewed sense of peace and clarity came over me. It proved to be a pivotal point in my life, where I started to define myself spiritually, and in all ways really.

I was 52 in 2004, and one of the realizations that came out of that trial by fire was that it would be an uphill battle to be able to retire by or before 65, even with careful money management, a decent income and no health problems. This was a sobering thought, but also one that I was determined to overcome. After all, Colonel Sanders was 65 when he started Kentucky Fried Chicken!

According to a 2011 Statistics Canada report, **9.6** million Canadians (29%), are Baby Boomers.

As of April, 2014 data from the U.S. Census Bureau shows that there are **76.4** million baby boomers.

Born between 1946 and 1964, as of 2015 they range in age from 51 to 69.

At the time of writing these words, I am 62 and there have been many positive changes, including the state of my finances, since that day sitting by the river 10 years ago. I still need to keep working though, and learned that I have unwittingly joined the growing ranks of Baby Boomers that can't afford to, or don't want to, retire ("un-retired") by or before the traditional age of 65. "Un-retirement" is the growing trend away from earlier retirement, by choice or economic necessity, towards continuing to work past the age of 65. This guidebook focuses on un-retired Boomers.

Results from the Ipsos Reid poll conducted for the 2014 Sun Life Canadian Unretirement Index[1] found that: "As we have seen in past years, those who plan to work past 65 fall into two camps. Thirty-five per cent say they'll do so because they want to. Sixty-five per cent feel they will need to. The gap between the two has been gradually widening since 2011."

In the US, labor market participation rates of people 65 years and older has increased and according to the United States Census Bureau (2013): "Within the 65 and over population, 65 to 69-year-olds saw the largest change, increasing from 21.8 percent in 1990 to

30.8 percent in 2010, a 9.0 percentage point increase, compared with a 5.0 percentage point increase for 70- to 74-year-olds and a 1.0 percentage point increase for people 75 years and older."[2]

I decided that I would learn as much as I could about retirement and "un-retirement" in order to write this guidebook. This undertaking has taken me roughly 21 months to research; starting with the library and on-line sources, and branching into interviews with family and friends, those in my career network, entrepreneurs and random conversations with people whom I have run into.

I live on Vancouver Island where there is no shortage of Boomers to interview. The area attracts retirees due to its mild winters, affordable real estate and natural beauty. It is also inhabited, in part, by older workers that are unretired like myself.

Additionally, in communities throughout the US and Canada, I would like to acknowledge those large numbers of workers whose jobs don't pay enough to meet their present needs, let alone set aside money for retirement. They work in minimum wage, and/or part time jobs and may supplement their income with seasonal Employment Insurance or other government benefits. Many of these workers will remain un-retired because there is no other choice, working in jobs they may not like, without health benefits or employer pension plans. Their pension plans will rely on social security programs. Hopefully the economic gap that exists and is widening will be decreased by the efforts of those in positions of power in the near future.

I've been employed for the last 18+ years in career counselling initially, and later I advanced into rehabilitation counselling, which involves assisting individuals with medical conditions return to work. I presently have the privilege of working in the forest industry with its unionized members, who are often Baby Boomers.

As a result of my role, I have become deeply aware of how drastically injury, illness and other unexpected events can affect retirement goals.

A scenario I may encounter is when an individual in their fifties acquires an illness or injury that disables them from continuing to work in their physically demanding job. On top of this, there can be a long wait to get medical treatment, with savings becoming depleted along the way and retirement plans cut short. If the disability is significant and long term, the individual's earning years may be over and their standard of living is either fixed or decreases.

The men and women I work with are hardy and resilient and many that experience temporary setbacks from injury or illness, recover and return to work. Working as a rehabilitation counsellor has emphasized to me the importance of health and wellness to our quality of life, including the ability to earn money.

It doesn't matter whether your collar is blue or white, unretired Boomers come from all occupations and income levels. Besides the spectre of poor health or disability, there are also reasons for un-retirement that are common to all workers including being part of what is being described as the most challenging economic climate since the 1930's.

White collar workers (those that perform professional, managerial, or administrative work) may have more formal education, and a higher working income, but they are not excluded from un-retirement. These workers can find themselves impacted by global market changes, forced layoff, or job loss for other causes with their retirement savings interrupted. The news media is filled with numerous stories:

- offshoring of white collar jobs and in some cases moving entire companies overseas;
- corporate downsizing and the resulting reduction of management positions; and
- automation through digital technologies with job redundancy or loss.

For me, un-retirement feels like a race that hinges on my health and ability to stay employed and earn. Although I keep fit and live well,

I'm aware that it'll be best if I win the race *sooner rather than later.* I want to continue working into my "third age," but not have the type of work I do dictated by an urgent need to earn income.

If I no longer "must" work, and have enough savings to maintain a standard of living that I am okay with, then I have won the race.

There is more to working however, than just earning money.

In the course of researching and writing this book, I learned about and met many happy (successful) un-retirees. I discovered that there are compelling and healthy reasons to keep on working such as:

- enhancing our wellbeing as we engage in challenging and meaningful work;
- supporting healthy aging through social connection, which reduces isolation, loneliness and related mental health issues;
- reducing age discrimination by provably dismissing the notion that by 65 we are no longer useful or employable;
- providing the opportunity to keep learning new skills; and
- having an opportunity to be part of an exciting, evolving, diverse workforce.

Additional to the benefits of working is the expectation that there will be a demand for able older workers: "Older Canadians are an important source of labor supply. Governments and workforce experts agree that the labor force participation of older workers will be essential for future economic prosperity."[3]

10 benefits of delaying retirement as described by Emily Brandon (2013) (paraphrased)[4:]

1. Maybe you like your job; it brings its own rewards, so why leave it?

2. There will be no shortage of money.

3. I do not want to change my standard of living

4. Working longer may make me less susceptible to dementia.

5. I value the friendships I have in the workplace.

6. Time spent at work and away from home allows for a better balance in my marriage.

7. By working longer I will continue to contribute to my private and government pensions.

8. Allows me to hold off on paying taxes longer on my investments.

9. There are benefits through my employer such as disability and health insurance.

10. I enjoy providing a service and collaborating with others.

There are several reasons for this projection that include: older workers retiring; a skills gap; and the *difference* in the replacement population size between Boomers and incoming younger generations.

These changes in the labor market are redefining what retirement looks like in the years ahead and creating opportunities for those un-retirees who remain relevant and current.

This guidebook is partly my story, and it mirrors that large cohort of unretired Boomers who never fit into the financial industry's "freedom 50 plus" model. This is due to the many unexpected personal and market events and circumstances that can prevent financial freedom or on the other hand the need to retire at a set age, from occurring.

My intent is to educate, and humbly "light the way" for

those older workers facing the uncertainty of un-retirement. The four main areas that unretired Boomers need to understand and manage are:

1. **Standard of Living**
2. **Health and Wellness**
3. **Age Discrimination**
4. **Staying Gainfully Employed**

The Un-Retirement Guide™ offers information, strategies and tools to survive and thrive in un-retirement. Knowledge is power, and by breaking down the big picture into its parts you can create a Complete Life Wellness Plan™ that identifies where you are now and how best to get to your destination.

Happily, as a part of my journey, I discovered that continuing to work is good for your health and wellness, especially if it is aligned with your values and interests, and provides a useful service to others. Of course it should meet your financial needs while doing so, or be a step in that direction.

For unretired Boomers striving to reach financial independence, it can be difficult not to worry and/or fixate on this pursuit. Part 2 and 3 of this guidebook advises how to create wellness in the seven dimensions (including the occupational) and as a result produce greater balance in our lives.

I have included background on the origin of retirement and its relationship to age discrimination and other useful things to know, in the short upcoming chapter.

FASCINATING FACTS ABOUT RETIREMENT, OR THE LACK THERE OF

Chapter Two

It is better to live rich than to die rich
Samuel Johnson

Before we go much further, it makes sense to discuss the concept and history of retirement. When I conducted my extensive research over 21 months, I discovered that there was a lot about retirement that I didn't know.

It is interesting to me that prior to the late 1800's, people didn't retire. They worked until they couldn't anymore, and then died, usually a lot earlier than they may have liked.

"In the developed countries, the fragmentary data that is available suggest that life expectancy at birth was around 35 to 40 years in the mid-1700s, that it rose to about 45 to 50 by the mid-1800s, and that rapid improvements began at the end of the nineteenth century, so that by the middle of the twentieth century it was approximately 66 to 67 years. Since 1950 gains in life expectancy have been smaller, approximately eight more years have been added."[1]

In North America, mandatory retirement at a certain age did not exist until the mid-1800's.

Chappell, Gee et al (2003) describe how: "Retirement did not exist in the pre-industrial agrarian era up to the 1840s. Instead, older men and women "stepped down" from their former participation in the work force to take on less onerous work, receive care from their families, or decline into poverty. The industrial revolution between the 1840s and 1930s caused a transformation in Canada from a rural agrarian society to an urban industrial one. It was during this time that retirement began to take shape as an institutionalized phase of the life course, and with it a change from competence to age as the bureaucratic criterion used by employers as the reason for exit from the labor force."[2]

The origin of a mandatory age for retirement is attributed to the Iron Chancellor, Otto von Bismarck of Germany. "He introduced a social security system to appeal to the German working class and combat the power of the Socialist Party in Germany during the late 1800's. Somewhat cynically, Bismarck knew that the program would cost little because the average German worker never reached 65, and many of those who did lived only a few years beyond that age. When the United States finally passed a social security law in 1935 (more than 55 years after the conservative German chancellor introduced it in Germany), the average life expectancy in America was only 61.7 years." (Schulz, 1988) [3]

The implications of an age-based retirement policy are depicted in this quote from (CARP, 2008): "Mandatory retirement is a forced termination of employment solely based on age, not on a person's individual ability to perform the work. When the government's action does not take any consideration of individual's actual needs, capacities, and circumstances, it amounts to substantive discrimination. Therefore, mandatory retirement is clearly a form of age discrimination." [4]

A major and progressive change in Canadian retirement policy was bought into effect when: "On December 15, 2012, the federal government's repeal of the mandatory retirement exemption in the Canadian Human Rights Act came into effect, completing, with notable exceptions, the nation-wide ban of mandatory retirement that commenced with repeal legislation introduced in Manitoba and Quebec in the 1970's. The federal sector was the last jurisdiction to eliminate mandatory retirement." [5]

The foundation for working later in our lives is being built and underway. An Alberta, Canada employer survey (2012) comments on the increase of mature workers in the workforce:

"While many *positive* factors, such as:

- increased life expectancy;
- better health;
- and higher education levels may be the reason older workers are choosing to stay in the labor force into their senior years,

several *negative* factors, such as:

- the most recent economic downturn;
- higher personal debt;
- and inadequate retirement savings

may be deterring these older workers from retiring." [7]

Employers in Canada and the U.S.A. have largely abolished mandatory retirement and opened the gates for unretired Boomers to keep working. What remains is possible age discrimination which will vary in degree, depending on the work setting. Coping with this barrier is discussed in Chapter 14.

Unretired Boomers can now legally work past 65 years of age and this is in step with the costs of living longer. "A century ago the duration of retirement was expected to be only a few years, and many people never lived long enough to experience it. It is interesting to consider that given the increases in human longevity, retirement can potentially last as long as our working life. *"The biggest financial risk we face in retirement today is outliving our savings; a century ago the biggest retirement risk was dying too young."* (Alger, 2013) [6]

In addition, with the end of mandatory retirement, an increasing number of less physically strenuous occupations and businesses facing labor shortages have contributed to the rising presence of older workers in the workplace.

The reasons that many Boomers didn't accumulate adequate assets to be able to retire are numerous: periods of unemployment; the impact of divorce and child support; costs for adult and grandchildren or ailing parents; living beyond our means and related lack of savings; being stuck in low paying jobs; taxation; inflation and the list goes on.

It is apparent that the bank slogan of "freedom 50 plus" does not work for everyone, and that unretired Boomers have been at the mercy of economic, social, health and labor market forces often outside of their control. Those with low literacy, the disabled, aboriginals, the elderly, single women and parents, and immigrants may be particularly hard hit.

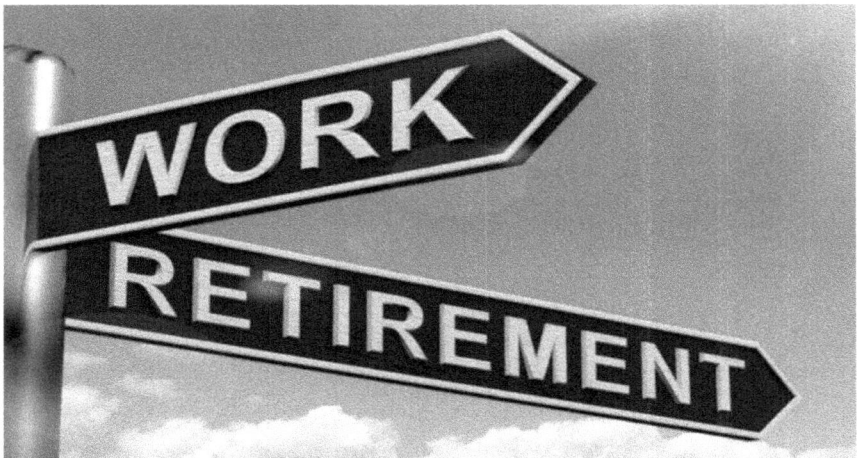

Zoomer Media Limited (2012) informs us "Data from Statistics Canada and the US Bureau of Labor Statistics confirms that a growing number of people are not retiring at age 65. In Canada, the percentage of participation in the labor force by people age 55 and up is at an all-time high. Experts believe the trend will continue, permanently wiping out the idea that 65 is a magic number signifying the end of the income-earning years. In both Canada and the USA, about 30% of people aged 65-69 are still working, either full time or part time. That age break captures only a tiny percentage of Baby Boomers, the oldest of whom just entered retirement age. The rest of the wave – now aged 47 to 64 – are still outside that traditional retirement benchmark. What will they do when they hit the number? The research is clear: they'll keep right on working."[8]

Boomers may continue to work to contribute and stay connected, but significant numbers will do so out of economic necessity. Bestselling author Kimberly Foss (2013), advises "Saving up enough money to pay for a 30-year retirement is a daunting prospect. Many Americans don't have enough money to retire in this ultra-low interest rate environment."[9]

From the perspective of an exercise in arithmetic, working into our late 60's or 70's might be the point where savings are enough to retire. There are however, other significant aspects involved that will influence how long we work.

What might Boomers value the most in the remainder of their life? The results of a recent study in the USA found that: "Health is the most important ingredient for a *happy* retirement, according to 81% of retirees. Meanwhile, paying for health care costs is Americans' greatest financial concern. The study explores three major forces that are redefining how individuals plan for health in retirement, including:

- an empowered Baby Boomer generation of health care consumers;
- the potential rise of chronic disease due to longer life spans; and
- how longevity is causing *health and wealth* to converge like never before." *(Merrill Lynch, Age Wave, 2014).*[10]

Paying for ongoing health care costs is a financial concern for unretired Boomers across North America and around the world wherever its aging members are increasing as a percentage of the total population.

If we proactively manage our health and careers while aging, I believe that we can remain engaged and successful. Interestingly, Brandon (2013) cites a study by the French National Institute of Health and Medical Research, in conjunction with the Bordeaux School of Public Health. The 2013 study of about 429,000 self-employed workers in France found people who retire later have a lower risk of developing dementia. [11]

It requires a split mindset to earn and save enough money to live on in the present and retire with at a future point. During our working lives we are expected to follow a budget, financially plan and increase our net worth. Our income along the way may not be enough to cover our present and future needs and be a chronic stressor we live with for years.

Unretired Boomers know the feeling of working hard to achieve financial security. We need to keep the wolves away from the door in the present and future, but at the same time our lives can change at any moment due to unplanned events like the global economy, or personal ones such as illness or disability.

Ahead is Chapter 3 on standard of living, which is related to comfort, net worth and financial security.

I believe that true security is an internal quality of peace and acceptance of what is going on day by day. We need to plan the best we can, but also accept each day on its own terms.

"It is through gratitude for the present moment that the spiritual dimension of life opens up."
Eckhart Tolle

WHAT STANDARD OF LIVING DO YOU WANT/DREAM OF?

Chapter Three

It is not the standard of living that is important,
but the manner of living.
Sri Sathya Sai Baba (Indian Spiritual leader, b.1926)

I know individuals and couples that have retired with no money concerns and maintain a high standard of living. Extensive travelling for some, and the ability to participate in a wide range of leisure activities make up their lifestyles. For those with grandkids, the younger generation becomes an important focus in their lifestyle. I've been told it is a warm feeling of relief when the need to earn money is gone. These retirees can lay back and use their time as they please. A common issue that does arise with my retired friends though, is their continued search to find meaning and purpose. Those that were employed before retiring often miss the structure and connection working provided.

My present standard of living is comfortable and one I'm making efforts to sustain long-term. If the plug was pulled on my primary job, I would need to find another source of income to prevent a reduction in my standard of living. I am, however, not motivated to scrimp along in order to create a nest egg for some future point I may never live to realize! I try to both save, enjoy and fund my leisure activities without squandering money. I have learned about managing money both personally and professionally and recognize the importance of financial literacy. I'm plugging along doing all that I can to increase my net worth, part of which is reinventing myself as an author. Where I end up is largely in the hands of God, so we shall see!

My lifestyle dream is: to winter outside of Canada from November to March, travelling to various tropical locales and spend the remaining months on beautiful Vancouver Island. I enjoy learning about different cultures and seeing new plants and animals. I will continue to write whatever my financial situation is, or wherever I live as I have found it gives me a sense of purpose and meaning. I believe that this will endure as I age, it isn't easy though! Lastly on this note, I realize what I want may not be for everyone.

I believe that financial abundance (having sufficient income to comfortably meet present needs and prepare reasonably for old age) is our birthright, although it is often not actualized.

George Miller (2013) investment expert and author of *Retirement Reboot*, describes 4 retirement lifestyles (or standards of living) that individuals may achieve, or aspire to. He says:

"Let's be optimistic and assume you will live long enough to retire, as most of us will. There are four levels of retirement lifestyles:

1. **Subsistence lifestyle**, where you must live on Social Security and welfare.
2. **Have-to-have lifestyle**, in which you have adequate income and resources for the basics, but not much else.
3. **Comfortable lifestyle**, which includes travel, visiting family, pursuing hobbies, and whatever else, turns you on, within limits.
4. **Luxurious lifestyle**, which may include multiple residences, extensive travel, fine dining, charitable giving, etc."[1]

Note that an increase in income does not necessarily result in a lasting increase in happiness. According to Brickman and Campbell (1971) [2], as a person makes more money, typically their expectations and desires also rise in tandem, which results in no permanent gain in happiness. This is known as hedonic adaptation.

That said, those individuals at the lowest level of subsistence (living at or below the poverty line), may live out their days there. If winning the race is to become financially independent, then those of us, that end up with a subsistence lifestyle have definitely not "won the race."

"Poverty" is defined as a state or condition in which a person lacks the financial resources and essentials to enjoy a minimum standard of living and well-being that is considered acceptable by society." [3] This standard is set by *Statistics* Canada's (2010) [4] in their low income cut-off thresholds. The low income cut-off after tax for a household size of 1 person living in a metropolitan area of over 500,000 inhabitants (i.e. Toronto) is $18,759 per annum gross income from all sources. This level of income is subject to adjustment and will increase as inflation increases. This works out to $1563.25 per month gross, to survive in a large city in 2010.

Poverty in Canada and the USA, let alone globally is the topic of another book.

For those striving to live above a subsistence level, there are three key areas that need to be addressed:

1. What will your cost of living be, given the lifestyle you want?
2. What income streams will you have?
3. What will your net worth be?

1. Cost of Living

Investopedia advises that the "Cost of living is the amount of money needed to sustain a certain level of living, including basic expenses such as housing, food, taxes and healthcare. Cost of living can be a significant factor in personal wealth accumulation because a smaller salary can go further in a city where it doesn't cost a lot to get by, while a large salary can seem insufficient in an expensive city."[5]

2. Income

Income is one of the single most important factors influencing quality of life in general. It is a key indicator of wellbeing and health for individuals, household and communities. Income levels indicate the ability of people to purchase essential and non-essential goods and services including food, housing, health services and transport.[6]

Unretired Boomers are at varying points on the road to financial independence and for many, continuing to earn money is necessary. During the course of our careers, we typically derive income from working as an employee or through self-employment.

Human Resources and Skills Development Canada Report on Housing (2010)[9]

The majority of Canadians have access to suitable, adequate, and affordable housing. However, in 2006 close to 13% of households lived in housing that was too small for the number of members in their household, was in need of major repair, or was too costly given their means.

Renters and those with incomes less than $27,607 per year were much more likely to be unable to find adequate, suitable, and affordable housing in 2006 than were owners and/or households with higher incomes. Aboriginal, lone-parent, and recent immigrant households as well as individuals living alone were also more likely to experience housing problems.

In 2008, the rate of new housing starts in Canada was 56 per 10,000 Canadians. Starts were highest in Alberta and Newfoundland and Labrador, where there were 68 new housing starts for every 10,000 residents.

Rental vacancy rates have increased since 2001, and reached a national average of 2.9% in 2010. Among Canada's 15 largest urban areas, eight had rental vacancy rates below the national average.

As we age, and if we accumulated assets, there can be the opportunity to receive money from passive or residual income. If we produce adequate funds from passive or residual income to cover living and leisure expenses, our time could be spent performing activities not driven by earning. What might that look like?

3. Net Worth

Employment and Social Development Canada (2005) advises that "Net worth, also referred to as wealth, is one measure of an individual's *material* well-being. It is the amount by which assets differ from liabilities or debt. Net worth represents the degree of flexibility Canadians have to respond to unexpected events (such as a job loss), or to opportunities (such as starting a business), or needs that arise (such as paying for a child's education). Building up net worth is also a key part of retirement planning, enabling a more comfortable retirement."[7]

Optimally, Boomers are able to maintain a comfortable standard of living while working and also when they stop. Industry Fund Services (2014)[8] in Australia determined that "A comfortable lifestyle in retirement would enable an individual to be involved in a broad range of leisure and recreational activities and to have a good standard of living through the purchase of items such as household goods, private health insurance, a reasonable car, good clothes, a range of electronic equipment and domestic and occasionally international travel."

Unretired Boomers work longer in their efforts to maintain and/or achieve a sustainable and comfortable lifestyle. How long this takes depends on the individual's career and financial circumstances. It is important not to forget that the state of our heath is the wildcard in this timeline and will be discussed in Part 2.

As previously mentioned, The Un-Retirement Guide™ doesn't focus on financial planning as there are many books written on this subject. It is important, though, that a well thought out financial plan is in place and followed and as we have heard before, the earlier the better.

Calculate the monthly cost of your standard of living

Please go to **Appendix A**, to calculate the monthly cost of your standard of living. This is based on **essential** (non-optional) costs, or what you NEED to live, as well as **discretionary** expenses, or what you would LIKE to have to maintain your current standard of living. A monthly and yearly total is obtained and serves as the amount of net income you will need to maintain your current *standard of living*. This can also be adjusted for inflation each year, as of 2014 it is approximately 2% for both the USA and Canada.

Once you know what you NEED and would LIKE, then you have the facts to plan accordingly.

A key element of retirement planning is to eliminate credit card and other high interest debt.

If you pre-maturely stop working due to job loss, disability or other reason and the amount of combined income from your savings, pensions, passive income is less than what you earned while employed, a trimming of expenses will be required.

Housing cost, the largest and perhaps least flexible component of a household budget, is also an important factor in the *financial security* of Canadian households. For many unretired Boomers housing presents a major expense either with ongoing mortgage or rent payments. Owning your residence outright may be the best position to be in, although tying up all your net worth in a house gets mixed reviews from the financial community.

What can you do if your current income/savings ability and net worth will not support the lifestyle that you want?

There are several options:

- The costs for essential expenses such as housing can be decreased for a couple versus single Boomers or as an extended family. By combining government pension, old age security payments, savings and/or investments a more comfortable lifestyle can be maintained.

- Many unretired Boomers are choosing to live in countries that offer a good standard of living combined with a lower cost of living. This is not for everyone, but with the use of technology to stay connected and/or work remotely, it may offer a viable solution.
- Reduce and eliminate debt.
- Sell your existing home and downsize into more affordable accommodation.
- Continue to work longer in your latest job or alternate one and phase in retirement to increase your savings.
- Reinvent yourself to create additional income.
- Minimize income taxes, adjust your portfolio for greater returns or take other actions to reduce costs and increase net worth.

Standard of living implies comfort, security and degrees of wealth.

Next we move onto our most valuable asset, health.

The upcoming chapters in Part 2 explore the differences between health and wellness, and why health is "not merely the absence of disease or infirmity."

The Un-Retirement Guide™ supports that choosing and practicing a wellness lifestyle is the best route to meet our overall needs and that no particular reason is necessary for a celebration!

Part 2
Investing in your Future

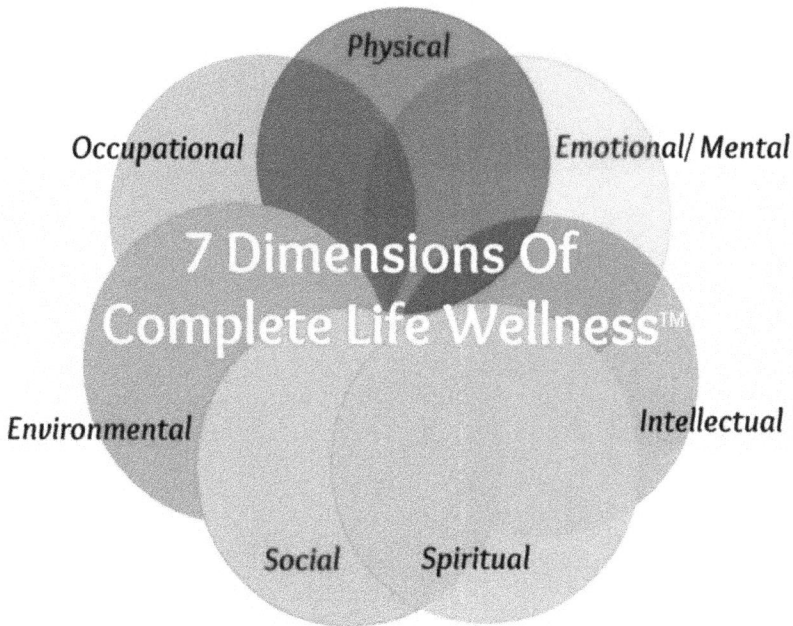

Physical

Occupational

Emotional/ Mental

7 Dimensions Of Complete Life Wellness™

Environmental

Intellectual

Social   Spiritual

BEHIND THE SCENES
WITH HEALTH AND WELLNESS

Chapter Four

Take time for your health today or you will not have health for your time tomorrow
Irish Proverb

Over the last decade I have become more aware of the time and energy required to create my dream lifestyle. This includes continuing to work at my full time job, and additional efforts to develop other streams of income. In hindsight, I have found out that the ability to persevere and commit to achieving these goals is part of who I am!

The cliché that health is the key that allows us to pursue wealth rings true. Injury, disease or illness can occur at any age, but for older workers the probability of this occurring is greater. Health is truly our greatest asset whether we need to work or not.

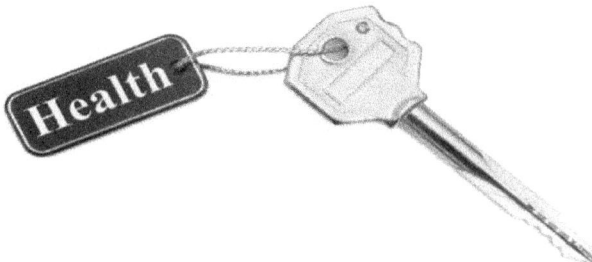

The unretired Boomers discussed next, find themselves facing very different circumstances, based upon the way they have lived their lives:

Fred worked as a personal injury lawyer, often 60 hours per week, and was respected for the results he produced. He was desk-bound for years, all the while working in a high pressure environment. Significant weight gain, chronic stress-related symptoms including insomnia and irritability, a lack of exercise and poor nutrition resulted in a health crisis for Fred. At 55, the age he was considering retiring, he suffered a major heart attack, resulting in open heart surgery and was also diagnosed with diabetes, high blood pressure and later reactive depression, all requiring medication and lifestyle changes to control. Fred has disability insurance but required a lengthy recovery and without his high working income to cover the overhead, combined with recent stock market losses, he now finds himself needing to stay employed years longer. Fred has medical restrictions regarding the number of hours he works, which means he potentially earns less.

John and Mary are both unretired Boomers in their early 60's and have "aged well" as the saying goes. They have low stress jobs they enjoy, in the tourism industry and estimate they need to keep working to the end of their 60's to reach financial independence. John informed me that they are developing other streams of income to add money to the pot and try to balance working with adequate leisure time. Mary and John continue to upgrade themselves in their jobs to remain current, relevant and employable. They understand the importance of health and the need to be proactive in looking after it.

The daily choices we make that comprise our lifestyles have a bearing on whether we will reach our financial and other life goals.

Why Wellness?

A disabling medical condition can end our ability to earn income and negatively impact our quality of life. The statistics are staggering.

A report by the National Seniors Council (2013)[1] details the following statistics that are worth considering: "Over 40% of Canadians over the age of 65 report having a disability and this can refer to *chronic, prolonged or episodic illness or those who have sustained an injury.* As people age there is an increased risk for onset of a number of chronic diseases and or injuries. The chronic diseases most noted as impacting functional capacity include cancer, diabetes, musculoskeletal diseases and chronic obstructive pulmonary disease.

Individual health has a significant effect on early retirement and workforce participation. In 2011 illness/disability was the most reported reason provided by older adults aged 55-64 (17.2%) and seniors over the age of 65 (9.3% percent) for leaving a job in the previous year. "Among adults between 55-64 years of age and not in the workforce, but who wanted to work, 30% stated that they did not look for work due to illness in 2011."

Each of us is susceptible to periods of illness or frailty and eventually dying which is a natural part of our life cycle. The state of our health and longevity is influenced by the following variables:

1. **Genetics.** The National Academy of Science (2006) states that: "Although there are many possible causes of human disease, family history is often one of the strongest risk factors for common disease complexes such as cancer, cardiovascular disease (CVD), diabetes, autoimmune disorders, and psychiatric illnesses."[2]

2. **Medical Care.** Regular health screenings and becoming an active partner (self-care) with your doctor to manage your health can help prevent disease.

3. **Other.** This includes accidents, victims of violence, workplace accidents and falls in the home. Unmanaged stress and its relationship to disease and accidents are discussed in the following excerpt by de Jong (2007): "Stress is linked to the six leading causes of death – heart disease, cancer, lung ailments, *accidents*, cirrhosis of the liver, and suicide. The Occupational Safety and Health Administration has declared stress a hazard of the *workplace*."[3]

4. **Social Circumstances.** Powerful influences on our health are derived from circumstances such as education, income, housing, employment, poverty, crime, and other community forces. Robbins et al (2011)[4]

5. **Environmental Conditions.** Home, work, and community environments sometimes present us not only with barriers to active lifestyles but also with toxic hazards. Environmental pollutants, chemical contaminants, radon, occupational hazards, and tobacco smoke all have the potential for triggering cellular changes. Robbins et al (2011)[5]

6. **Lifestyle Behaviours.** A new report from The Centers for Disease Control and Prevention finds that: "people can live longer if they practice one or more healthy lifestyle behaviors — not smoking, eating a healthy diet, getting regular physical activity, and limiting alcohol consumption. Not smoking provides the most protection from dying early from all causes."[6]

The 6 categories above combine and are interactive in effect and account for an individual's susceptibility to disease and or injury. It is our lifestyle *behaviours* (50%) that, according to McGinnis (2003): "are the largest factor in our health and longevity."[7]

In an article titled "Genes vs. Lifestyle: What Matters Most for Health?" Peter Jaret shares the following; "Even if a condition like heart disease runs in your family, you can do a lot to break that pattern. Your choices and lifestyle make a big difference. Some genes lead to disease. "But for most people, a healthy lifestyle trumps inherited risk," says cardiologist Donald Lloyd-Jones."[8]

So even with a predisposition to a disease, we may inhibit the onset by our lifestyle choices and behaviours.

It is apparent then, that the style we live our life can be detrimental to our state of our health. We may develop one of the chronic diseases related to lifestyle that include: heart disease, cancer, stroke, type 2 diabetes, atherosclerosis, obesity and osteoporosis. These diseases develop over many years and are strongly influenced by lifestyle. According to Robbins et al (2011) "Chronic diseases account for not only 70 percent of all deaths in the United States but also cause major limitations in daily living for 1 out of 10 Americans."[9]

The Un-Retirement Guide™ supports that the best way to simplify and manage our health and longevity is by choosing a wellness lifestyle. An article from the Journal of the American Medical Association (AMA) noted that, in one research study, the "wellness" approach produced a 17% decline in total medical/ doctor visits and a 35% reduction in medical/doctor visits for minor illness. The participants in this study took part in a year-long self-care education program."[10]

Wellness Proposals 10, a wellness consulting company, concludes that: "Research studies related to wellness indicate that Americans who take good care of themselves and make healthy lifestyle choices are healthier, happier, more productive, miss work less, and have lower healthcare costs.[11]

A wellness lifestyle addresses more than disease prevention, it includes optimal health and positive wellness, which is discussed further in the remainder of this and the next chapter.

Definitions of Health and Wellness

Health is an elusive concept and its definition has evolved over many years. There is significant confusion regarding what Health and Wellness actually is.

Three leading approaches/models of Health include the:

1. Medical model
2. Holistic model
3. Wellness model

It is not within the scope of The Un-Retirement Guide™ to discuss theories of health in depth, so basic background only, will be given on the evolution of the Wellness model.

Using all three models gives us the best results and means, while recognizing the limitations of each. *The over-arching principle is that in addition to working with health professionals we're required to actively self-manage our own health and wellness needs.*

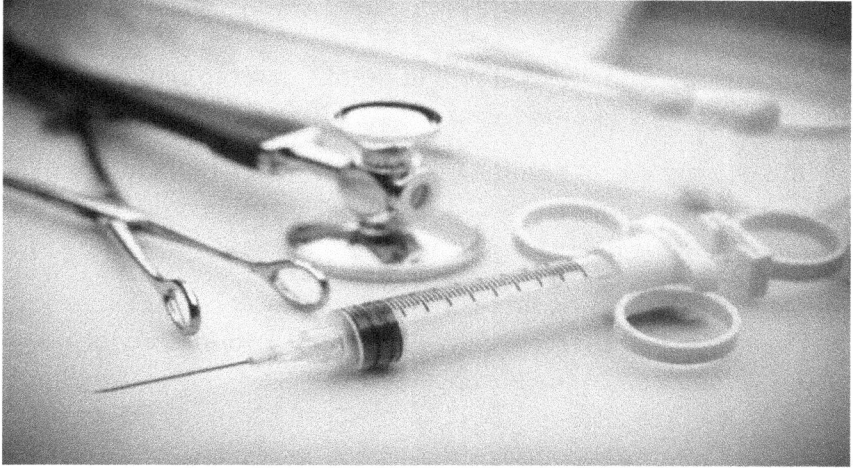

Medical Model

The medical model (allopathic) was dominant in North America throughout the 20th century.

Wikipedia comments that: "The concept of "disease" is central to the medical model. In general, "disease" refers to some deviation from normal body functioning that has undesirable consequences for the affected individual. An important aspect of the medical model is that it regards disease signs (objective indicators such as an elevated temperature) and symptoms (subjective feelings of distress expressed by the patient) as indicative of an underlying physical abnormality (pathology) within the individual."[12]

The medical model focuses on diseased organs and biological abnormalities. Health is regarded as the absence of disease. Obviously this model is critical in restoring health, but it tends to overlook psychological and social factors and other determinants of our health.

Holistic Model

The move from the medical definition of health to a more holistic model is portrayed in the following definition:

"In 1948 the World Health Organization (WHO) defined health as, "a state of complete physical, mental and social well-being and *not merely the absence of disease or infirmity.*"[13]

This definition views health as holistic, in that it is a *positive* state (wellbeing) experienced in our mind/body and interactions with others, in addition to the absence of disease.

Wellness Model

Not long after the work by the WHO, Robbins et al (2011) inform us that: "In the late 1950s Dr. Halbert Dunn began writing about the upper limits of health, the ultimate in health. He was the first to use the word wellness in his writings in reference to the pursuit of optimal well-being.

Dunn viewed "health" as a relatively passive and neutral state of existence—in contrast to "wellness," which he described as a never-changing process of growth toward an elevated state of superb well-being, and where one is actively working to reach it. Today, wellness is defined as an *integrated and dynamic level of functioning oriented toward maximizing potential, dependent on self-responsibility.*"[14]

There were other contributing wellness pioneers that followed in the 20th century, such as Dr. John W. Travis, who developed the concept that wellness exists on a continuum: "Wellness is never a static state. You just don't get well or stay well. There are many degrees or levels of wellness, just as there are degrees of illness." (Travis et al 2004)[15]

The development of a wellness model of health was further refined by the World Health Organization. Ian McDowell, on his health information site at the University of Ottawa writes: In 1984, a WHO discussion document proposed "moving away from viewing health as a state, toward a dynamic model that presented it as a process or a force."[16]

Beyond models and theories of wellness, let's end this chapter with a simple explanation of what wellness looks like in practice. The "National Wellness Institute devised three questions that can help persons and organizations assess the degree to which wellness is incorporated into a particular approach or program:

- Does this help people achieve their full potential?
- Does this recognize and address the whole person (multi-dimensional approach)?
- Does this affirm and mobilize peoples' positive qualities and strengths?"[17]

These three indicators of wellness are reframed and discussed again in the next chapter.

I have just skimmed the surface of how the wellness model of health evolved. I encourage you to research the topic of health to explore how central this concept is to our society. There are some great additional references suggested at the end of The Un-Retirement Guide™ in the notes for this chapter.

DESIGNING A WELLNESS LIFESTYLE

Chapter Five

Wellness is a lifestyle of self-responsibility that you choose and manage. It is a mindset that seeks change and growth. It is a dynamic, multi-dimensional process that includes not only the absence of disease by prevention, but also increased wellbeing, health and happiness.
Brian Lukyn

The Un-Retirement Guide™ supports that the following 3 components of Health can be enhanced by choosing and practicing a Wellness Lifestyle:

1. **Disease Prevention**
   - The incidence or effects of disease and or illness may be reduced.
2. **Complete, Optimal Health**

   - We are dynamic, multi-dimensional beings and symptoms of disease or illness are the result of an imbalance in these aspects of who we are. Optimal health is related to the integration of mind, body and environment.
3. **Positive Wellness**

   - By cultivating positive emotional-mental states (also known as happiness) we can improve our quality of life and promote longevity.

Happiness is not an unrealistic, fluffy concept. It has been pondered, and attempts to define it go back millennia. When the forefathers of the USA were drafting the Declaration of Independence in 1776 it was included as an inalienable right in Life, Liberty and the Pursuit of Happiness.

A spiritual system to achieve Happiness is a central theme in Buddhist teachings.

Wikipedia explains that: "Several humanistic psychologists—such as Abraham Maslow, Carl Rogers, and Erich Fromm—developed theories and practices pertaining to human happiness and flourishing. More recently, positive psychologists have found *empirical* support for the humanistic theories of flourishing. In addition, positive psychology has moved ahead in a variety of new directions."[1]

Disease prevention, optimal health and positive wellness (happiness) are all potential benefits of practicing a Wellness Lifestyle. But, how do we live this way? What is involved?

Dimensions, Needs and a Wellness Lifestyle

At the beginning of this chapter, I described Wellness as a lifestyle you choose and manage. This is an important concept that implies we're responsible for the actions we do or don't take as our lives unfold. The intent is not to strive for perfection but a steady, committed effort and growth towards optimal health and wellbeing. This doesn't mean that we live with our head in the sand or are unaware that living is risky business and undesirable events can happen that we have no control over.

We are multi-dimensional beings where each dimension overlaps and can work together, to create an integrated (the state of being whole and undivided) system. I should add that the dimensions can also work against each other as in the case of a chronic stress response.

As we are: "In the process of achieving or striving for holistic wellness (a journey, not an end-state), people come closer to satisfying their system of basic human needs." (McGregor 2010)[2]

I have developed **A Complete Life Wellness Plan™** for the purpose of managing our needs. It has a framework of seven dimensions that consist of the:

1. Physical
2. Emotional-Mental
3. Intellectual
4. Spiritual
5. Social
6. Environmental
7. Occupational

These seven dimensions are explored in detail in the upcoming Chapters (6-12). After reading through these chapters, you will gain a deeper sense of what the concepts multi-dimensional and holistic imply, and be better prepared to develop **A Complete Life Wellness Plan™.**

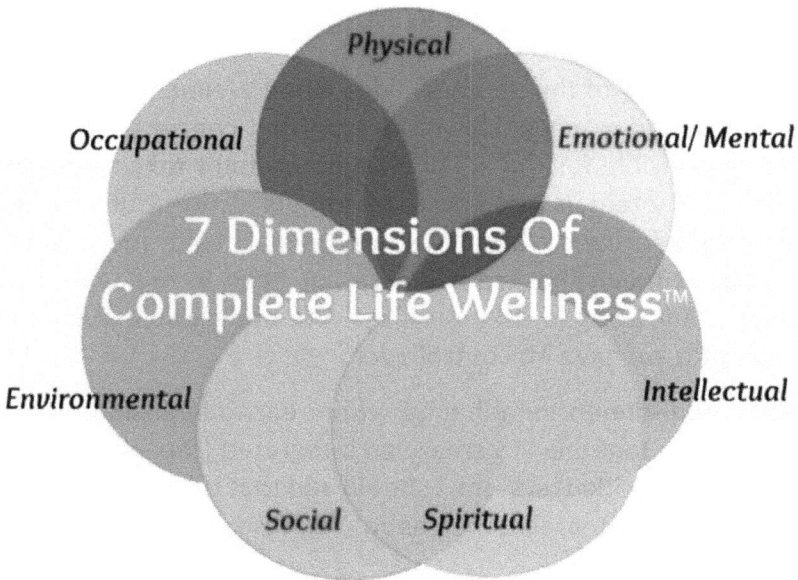

7 Dimensions Of Complete Life Wellness™

I recommend you read the rest of the guidebook first, before creating your **Complete Life Wellness Plan™**. To get a free Plan, go to http://brianlukyn.com/companion-eBook/ to download a copy.

Have patience, I believe the information that lies in the chapters ahead will educate, entertain and inspire!

The first of the seven dimensions and an important one to be discussed, is the physical and up next.

PHYSICAL WELLNESS

Chapter Six

Take care of your body. It's the only place you have to live.
Jim Rohn

I park my car one kilometer above the top end of the park and start out walking in an evergreen forest that has a spicy fragrance and continues down to the ocean.

The frothing white surf crashes onto the sandy beach with a deep powerful sound I feel inside my body. The scene before me is one aspect of an amazing marine park where I walk several times a week. Part of my route is beside the sea, and the other is to the top of the escarpment that juts up along its eastern edge.

This leg of my outing along the ocean and surf is the warm-up before circling back to begin the hill climb portion, which starts out with 145 stairs. I feel gratitude that my body allows me to do this, but some days I have to push myself to get here. It is the first section of my uphill route. When I reach the top of the stairs I continue to walk a short distance along flat ground until I come to a trailhead. From here it takes 15 minutes up through another forest to the top of the escarpment. When I reach the summit I'm treated to a panoramic view of the ocean, lagoon, spit and the mountain range in the background. There are often eagles and seabirds flying nearby at the same height as I stand. I'm aware of my increased heartbeat, the awesome sights, smells, sounds and a feeling that this is as good as it gets. The entire walk takes 50 minutes and I always feel physical, emotional/mental, environmental and spiritual renewal afterwards.

I see others walking or running along the way, so there is also a social connection over a shared healthy activity even if it is only a nod and or smile. By partaking in this simple activity, my state of wellbeing is palpable.

The term body-mind is commonly heard in wellness circles these days. The physical dimension concentrates on the body and the need to look after it. The mind part obviously resides in the body and some argue it is hard to know where one begins and the other ends!

Wellness in the physical dimension refers to a daily lifestyle that creates a foundation of habits that supports healthy body function and increases your odds of living a long, full life.

These **four foundational lifestyle habits** center on exercising our bodies, eating a nutritional diet, getting adequate sleep and, often overlooked, learning to consciously breathe. Let's look at these next and in doing so, perhaps increase our awareness and knowledge further, both also components of practicing a wellness lifestyle.

Exercise Matters

The research definitely supports the importance of exercise for healthy aging, and the need to challenge the notion that fitness is for the younger generations only.

As older workers, we are exposed to stereotypes about aging and faltering physical ability. Boomers may fall victim to these stereotypes and carry a feeling that it is all downhill from here, but the research suggests otherwise.

An article from the Alliance for Aging Research (2013) in the US advises: "exercise may well hold the key to the fountain of youth. Besides boosting longevity, getting fit is one of the most important steps older adults can take to maintain their mobility, independence and quality of life. Gone are the days when growing old gracefully meant slowing down and taking it easy.

For the 77 million baby boomers born between 1946 and 1964 it means just the opposite. Inactivity, not aging, is the culprit behind chronic conditions such as heart disease, obesity, and osteoporosis. The good news is, there is a lot you can do to delay or prevent them."[1]

Gretchen Reynolds (2011) writes in *O Magazine*; "Not long ago, most people—scientists included—were convinced that the biological indignities of aging were more or less inevitable. Survive past midlife and you'd start losing muscle mass, height, energy, and your car keys. Well, nuts to that. New and inspiring research shows that the supposed physical 'certainties' of aging are mostly avoidable. Muscles don't necessarily shrivel. You don't have to shrink or slow down. One word: Move. Even minimal amounts of exercise can counteract the effects of time."[2]

Research supports the physical benefits of continuing to work and this is a "silver lining" to the fact that many Boomers cannot afford to retire.

Peter Orszag (2013), in an article for Bloomberg writes; "Researchers at the Institute of Economic Affairs in the U.K. have also recently identified...negative and substantial effects on health from retirement." Their study found retirement to be associated with a significant increase in clinical depression and a decline in self-assessed health, and that these effects grew larger as the number of years' people spent in retirement increased. Similarly, a study published in 2008 by the National Bureau of Economic Research found that full retirement *increased difficulties with mobility and daily activities* by 5 percent to 16 percent and, by reducing *physical exertion* and social interactions, also harmed mental health."[3] These potential negative effects of retirement underline the need to focus on the physical dimension.

While it is critical to keep exercising our bodies, we need to be aware that as we age we're at increased risk of sustaining an injury while doing so. This is not an excuse not to keep moving, but requires more care in how we exercise. Taking time to warm up and slowly build the intensity and or length of exercise is essential to preventing sprains and strains, bursitis, tendonitis or worse. If we stay active several (3-5) days per week it will prepare us better for 18 holes of golf, a long bike ride, tennis or other activities than jumping in de-conditioned.

I've played sports, participated in martial arts, golfed, am a yogi, lifted weights, jogged long distances, and played squash and tennis over the years. I've also experienced several injuries to my knees and lower back and as a result more careful now in how I exercise.

These days, I have developed a balanced fitness program that includes my beach walk for cardiovascular exercise, light weight-lifting, high rep. strength training and yoga for flexibility and mindfulness. In a perfect week I do two of each activity for 6 days, which sounds like a lot but the weight training take 40 minutes of my day, the walk 50 minutes of another day and the yoga 90 minutes. Yoga is an ancient and worthwhile activity that improves my wellbeing and is a key piece of my fitness program. There are many misconceptions about yoga and if interested, I suggest you checking it out for yourself.

Design your own exercise program, **one you are comfortable doing and that you enjoy**. Keep the balanced aspect in mind I mentioned above and take steps to minimize the possibility of injury. Exercise is a great way to relieve stress and change our mood if need be.

Diet Matters Too

Diet, in combination with exercise, has a very significant influence on our state of health.

On the excellent InteliHealth website, it advises that: "The importance of good nutrition is nothing new. Back in 400 B.C., Hippocrates said, 'Let food be your medicine and medicine be your food.' Today, good nutrition is more important than ever.

At least 4 of the 10 leading causes of death in the U.S. — heart disease, cancer, stroke and diabetes — are directly related to the way we eat; diet is also implicated in scores of other conditions. But while the wrong diet can be deadly, eating right is among the cornerstones of health."[4]

Chronic diseases are prevalent in North America. These are the so called "lifestyle diseases" related to our eating and exercise habits. When I use the word eating or diet in this regard, it includes all of the substances that we take into our bodies.

"Heart disease, cancer, stroke, respiratory disease and diabetes are among the leading causes of death in Canada. Worldwide, these chronic conditions account for 60% of all deaths. Since they are influenced by modifiable behaviours, they are considered largely preventable. For people with a chronic illness, adopting a healthier lifestyle, such as smoking cessation, increased physical activity, eliminating heavy alcohol consumption and improving diet, can extend longevity, reduce the recurrence of an event and enhance quality of life."[5]

The Statistics Canada report that the excerpt above was taken from is the result of a 12-year longitudinal national population health survey. Tragically, the survey found that numbers of the participants over 50 were unable to make lifestyle changes, even after being diagnosed with a chronic disease.

It is never too late to make changes though, and move towards increased health and wellness!

Chronic diseases related to lifestyle and dietary patterns eventually kill. They may take years to develop, but also result in ongoing disability and major limitations in daily living. It is not my intent to present this information as a scare tactic but to illustrate the effect our lifestyle habits have on our quality of life.

A healthy diet (which includes adequate hydration) is an important component of wellbeing and: "How we feel can be a result of what we eat, but what we eat can also be due to how we are feeling. Food and the chemicals in our brains interact to keep us going throughout the day. It is important to eat a variety of healthy foods, as they have different effects on our brains. For example, carbohydrates increase serotonin, a brain chemical that has a calming effect. Perhaps that's why people often crave carbohydrate-rich foods when they are under stress. Protein-rich foods increase tyrosine, dopamine, and norepinephrine, which help to increase alertness. In addition, certain healthy fats (omega-3 fatty acids) become part of the membranes of brain cells and control many brain processes. Poor nutrition or lack of a variety of healthy foods can contribute to depression by limiting the availability of these specific nutrients." [6]

There is a confusing array of information regarding what to eat, some of which may have solely profit-motivated intent. I would speak to a naturopath or nutritionist if you are in doubt on what foods are best for you.

It takes planning to organize our meals. This is time well spent, but it requires effort. Food, especially organic food, is becoming expensive; I counter this by telling myself that it is a great investment in my health as I am paying for my order. We will not always be able to organize and eat nourishing meals and need to cut ourselves some slack in this regard, but not too much though! Mealtime as a social gathering where the focus is on connection and the shared need to eat is a simple way to increase our wellbeing.

Diet and exercise are two major lifestyle habits that influence our wellness in the physical dimension. The last two healthy habits of sleeping well and breathing properly add to our balance and health.

The Sleeping Habit

Why do we need to get adequate sleep each night? What happens during this apparent state of inactivity that makes it an important lifestyle habit to practice?

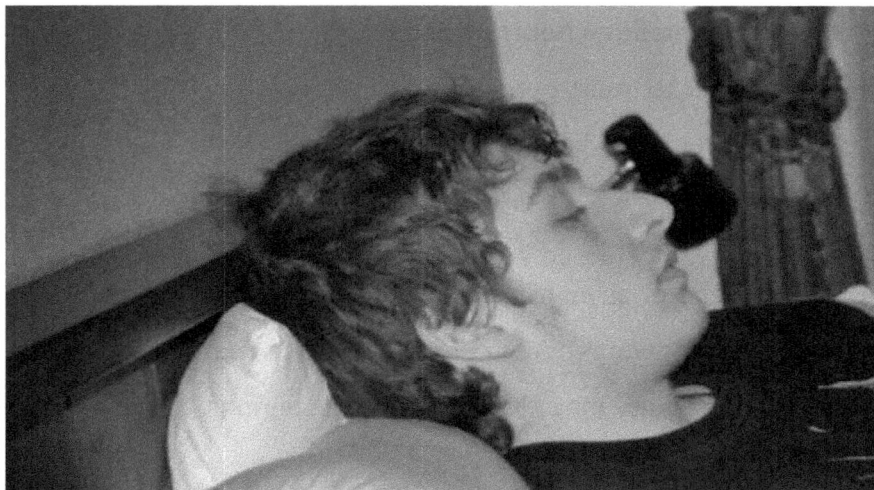

The National Sleep Foundation in the US advises: "We sleep to restore brain chemicals and rest the body. Some researchers believe that the brain organizes and stores memories during sleep.

Lack of sleep can affect our daytime functioning, hormonal balance, appetite, and immune system function." [7]

On a website produced by the Division of Sleep Medicine at Harvard Medical School and the WGBH Educational Foundation it is stated that: "Numerous studies have found that insufficient sleep increases a person's risk of developing serious medical conditions, including obesity, diabetes, and cardiovascular disease."[8]

Sleep hygiene refers to the habits and practices that enable us to sleep soundly on a regular basis and be alert during the day and: "The most important sleep hygiene measure is to maintain a regular wake and sleep pattern seven days a week.

It is also important to spend an appropriate amount of time in bed, not too little, or too excessive."[10]

Recommended hours of sleep:

Babies: 16 hours per day

Children: 9-16 hours per day

Teenagers: 9 hours per day

Adults: most need 7-8 hours, but some may need as few as 5 or as many as 10

Pregnant women need more sleep than usual

Older adults may sleep for shorter periods of time, more often.

The Depression and Bipolar Support Alliance[9]

Other examples of sleep hygiene practices are:

- practicing stress management if necessary;
- sleep in a dark room, not too hot or cold;
- buy a quality bed and pillows and comfortable bedding;
- don't go to bed hungry or stuffed;
- limit stimulants like caffeine to no later than the mid-afternoon or eliminate altogether;
- limit day time naps to the mid-afternoon and no longer than 30 minutes;
- make sure the bed is big enough and there is room for moving around during sleep;
- if your partners snore or hoards the covers, sleeping in separate beds or ear plugs may be necessary;
- have a bedtime routine where you focus on relaxing and winding down; and
- have a shower or bath to prepare for sleep.

Difficulties sleeping are common and most of us just don't get enough sleep. Over half of Canadians only get around seven hours of sleep a night, and say that they feel tired most of the time."[11]

The Wellness dimensions, of course, are all interactive. Our exercise and eating habits can influence our sleeping patterns. Cultivating positive sleep habits is very important to your overall health: "Many experts suggest that quality sleep is as important to your health and well-being as good nutrition and exercise is."[12]

Breathing Effectively

We can easily overlook breathing properly as important to health, because it is carried out unconsciously, but can also be performed consciously. How efficiently we breathe effects our body-mind.

Travis and Ryan (2004) inform us that: "Breathing is synonymous with living. It's basic to our energy-transforming metabolism. In the Wellness Energy System, breathing provides the first energy input. The oxygen that breathing provides is needed for the production of the high-energy chemical bonds that result when it combines with our blood sugar within every cell of our body."[13]

It is astounding to consider that: "We take approximately 15,000 breaths every day, and if we could breathe efficiently for only a small percentage of those breaths we would make a tremendous improvement in our physical, emotional and psychological well-being as well as enhancing our awareness of our spiritual selves – our soul – who we truly are."[14]

Andrew Weill MD, a wellness leader, posts on his excellent website that: "Most people do not know how to breathe so as to take full advantage of the nourishing, health-giving properties of the act of breathing. Knowing how to perform simple breathing techniques can help lower your blood pressure, calm a racing heart, or help your digestive system without taking drugs."[15]

Checking in with ourselves throughout the day to practice developing a diaphragmatic breathing habit, will influence how we age and is an important tool for stress management. I have learned this habit in my yoga practice, with the regular reminders supplied by the teachers to consciously belly breathe.

In this chapter we have discussed **THE 4 FOUNDATIONAL LIFE-STYLE HABITS** which are:

1. exercising our bodies
2. a nutritional diet
3. adequate sleep and
4. diaphragmatic breathing

Taking the time and effort to develop a foundation of healthy exercise, eating, sleeping and breathing habits is going to positively affect all seven dimensions. As our physical wellness is increased, another by-product is that our resilience to stressors is fortified.

Remember that once these habits are created they can become automatic!

Do the best you can for a particular day, a small action is better than none.

A summary of the brain/mind-body benefits derived from practicing **THE 4 FOUNDATIONAL LIFESTYLE HABITS** can be found on the last page of Chapter 8.

Due to the importance of understanding and minimizing the impact of stressors in our lives, it is discussed in the next chapter on the Emotional/Mental dimension, and again in Chapter 13.

EMOTIONAL/MENTAL DIMENSION

Chapter Seven

You must learn to let go. Release the stress.
You were never in control anyway.

Steve Maraboli, Life, the Truth, and Being Free

Learning to embrace and regulate our emotional dimension is a journey of self-discovery.

I like the definition of emotional wellness provided by Hales (2005) where he proposes that it: "includes trust, self-esteem, self-acceptance, self-confidence, self-control, and the ability to bounce back from setbacks and failures. Maintaining emotional wellness requires monitoring and *exploring your thoughts or feelings*; identifying obstacles to emotional well-being and finding solutions to emotional problems, if necessary with the help of a therapist."[1]

Emotions can be uncomfortable and hard to accept, or the opposite and change often. They are the body's messenger, signalling whether our needs are being fulfilled or not. (The terms "emotion" and "feeling" are used interchangeably in this chapter for the sake of simplicity).

Much of the unease we may experience day to day is related to the stressors in our lives. These stressors can come from outside sources and/or from what we feel and think.

HeartMath Inc. (2014), a leading researcher and educator in the field of stress, offers this perspective: "Stress comes from our perception and emotional *reactions* to an event or idea. It can be any feeling of anxiety, irritation, frustration, or hopelessness, etc.

Stress is not only created by a response to an external situation or event. A lot of daily stress is created by ongoing attitudes, that is, recurring feelings of agitation, worry, anxiety, anger, judgments, resentment, insecurities and self-doubt. These emotions are known to drain emotional energy while engaging in everyday life."[2]

Here is a scenario regarding unmanaged chronic internal stressors that resulted in negative consequences:

Several company restructurings later, found Jack working for a younger boss he had trained and who was less experienced and educated than he was. This was a political appointment, and Jack wasn't able to adapt to this unfair and radical change. He was fixated on the negative implications of his demotion and created a conspiracy narrative in his mind, where he became a powerless victim. Jack's smoking rate went up, he became unpleasant to be around and developed insomnia. Other symptoms showed up, like loss of appetite, irritability and an increase in aches and pains. Without knowing it, his prolonged reaction to these events turned into a chronic stress response, and a month later he went on medical leave.

Jack never returned to his former job and later reinvented himself into another career path. A large part of the chronic stress Jack experienced was due to the internal stressors of his thoughts and feelings.

According to Smith et al (2014): "Understanding the influence emotions have on your thoughts and actions are vital to managing stress. Life doesn't have to feel like a rollercoaster ride with extreme ups and downs. Once you're aware of your emotions, even the painful ones you normally try to avoid or bottle up, the easier it is to understand your own motivations, stop saying or doing things you later regret, gain renewed energy, and smooth out the ride."[3]

I have worked on my emotional/mental wellness and progressed over the years. I continue to learn about this dimension of who I am. Ongoing efforts to look after my body's needs and being aware of and managing the stressors in my life has allowed me to experience greater life satisfaction.

Let's start out by defining what stress is and how it can change the way we feel, think and act.

Not all stress is bad for you. It's a normal part of our existence. A certain level of stress is necessary to meet the demands of life. It's a short-term physiological response that gives us added mental clarity, and that subsides when the challenge has been resolved, after which we return to a normal state.

When stress is negative and becomes long term or chronic, however, it can cause problems. Ongoing illness or un-wellness may be due to the effect of chronic stressors encountered in our daily lives. This imbalance can pose serious health risks. It can present as lowered mood, fatigue, rumination of our thoughts, insomnia, addictions and other symptoms which diminish our quality of life.

Managing and/or minimizing stress will positively influence our health, wellness, and aging and can be learned. It should also be kept in mind that the way each of us responds to a stressor is different. The coping ability for one person may be different for another.

Un-retirement, and striving to achieve financial freedom can be a significant stressor for older workers. Unmanaged internal and/or external stressors can set the stage for disease and, en route, related degrees of illness.

Dr. Lazarus and Dr. Selye, who were both pioneers in stress research, determined that there are two types of stress:

- Eustress or positive stress; and
- Distress or negative stress.

Eustress or positive stress

- Is viewed as something we can handle
- Improves how we perform
- Motivates and focuses energy
- Is short term
- Feels exciting

Distress or negative stress, on the other hand

- Causes anxiety or worry
- Can range from short to long-term
- Is viewed as something we can't handle
- Feels unpleasant
- Decreases our performance
- Can lead to illness and or disease

The Un-Retirement Guide™ is concerned with managing distress or negative stress. Therefore, when the word "stress" is used in this chapter, it refers to negative stress. Let's explore the basics of this pervasive threat to our health, wellbeing and longevity.

> Essentially we "stress out" for three reasons;
>
> 1. Changes in our life have an unsettling effect
> 2. We are feeling challenged or threatened by an outside force
> 3. We experience a loss of control
>
> The Wellness Center for students at Santa Clara University, (an excellent resource)[4]

Stress is:

- the mind-body reaction to the demands of the world
- a response of the mind-body to internal and/or external stressors
- any event or condition in life that a person finds threatening, difficult to cope with or causes excess pressure

The Stress Response

There are two types of responses to stress, depending on whether it is short or long term in duration.

Acute Stress

This type of stress response most of us are familiar with. Stress management expert Elizabeth Scott (2014) provides the following explanation: "Acute stress is experi-

enced in response to an immediate perceived threat, physical, emotional or psychological. The threat can be real or imagined; it's the *perception of threat that triggers the response*. During an acute stress response, the autonomic nervous system is activated and the body experiences increased levels of cortisol, adrenalin and other hormones that produce an increased heart rate, quickened breathing rate, and higher blood pressure. Blood is shunted from the extremities to the big muscles, preparing the body to fight or run away. This is also known as the fight-or-flight response."[5]

Many events could trigger an acute stress response such as:

- Childbirth
- Being part of natural disaster such as an earthquake
- A car accident
- Being robbed
- Sudden loud noise
- Injuring ourselves
- A soldier engaged in combat
- The death of a spouse or family member
- Hospitalization and surgery
- Being fired without cause

All of us experience events in our lives from time to time that produce the intense acute stress response. Symptoms usually settle down fairly quickly, but can sometimes remain for several days.

The second type of response to stress is chronic.

Chronic Stress

If the body does not return to a relaxation state, we experience chronic stress, which is a state of *ongoing physiological arousal* associated with the stress response. Chronic stress is also defined as a state of prolonged tension from internal or external stressors, or a mixture of both.

The connection between chronic stress and anxiety, depression and the capacity of the brain to rewire itself is elaborated on below.

Smith et al (2014) describe the health risks of a chronic stress response in this excerpt from their website: "Long-term exposure to stress can lead to serious health problems. Chronic stress *disrupts* nearly every system in your body. It can raise blood pressure, suppress the immune system, increase the risk of heart attack and stroke, contribute to infertility, and speed up the aging process. Long-term stress can even rewire the brain, leaving you more *vulnerable* to anxiety and depression."[6]

The Sun Life Canadian Health Index Survey (2011)[7] published its results in a report called *The Burnout Factor: A Unique Look at Stress* and found: "We live in a culture of chronic stress, with a seemingly endless list of life demands. Prolonged periods of high stress levels are a risk factor for all forms of psychological illness, with a consensus among the medical community that *prolonged exposure to stress* is a predictor of chronic conditions like depression and anxiety related disorders."

HeartMath (2014) describes the effect of chronic stress on the brain: "Experts say an important factor in today's stress experience is that it's not just about the single incident type of stress that naturally follows trauma, illness, job change, or other major life event. For most people it's the wear and tear of daily life. What used to work for stress relief before may not be as effective today, because modern stress is more about the on-going levels people are experiencing. *Daily life stress can be difficult to change because of how the brain works. Through repeated experiences of stress, the brain learns to recognize the patterns of activity associated with 'stress' as a familiar baseline, and in a sense, it becomes normal and comfortable. Without effective intervention, stress can become self-perpetuating and self-reinforcing."*[8]

Chronic Stressors and the Transactional Model (sounds complicated but it's not)

The events, conditions and pressures that may trigger the stress response are known as stressors.

It is a common belief that stress is *caused by external situations, but the research performed has found otherwise.*

The theory that accounts for both the internal and external stressor is the Transactional Model. It theorizes that stress is caused by a transaction, where there is an interaction between the stressor, our view of the stressor and our perceived ability to cope with it.[9]

The model states: "It's our own internal beliefs, attitudes, interpretations, perceptions and other factors, in combination with the external events that tend to create stress"[10] Or put another way, we tend to create our own stress by how we react emotionally, mentally and the resulting actions we take to cope.

Both internal and external stressors require our attention.

Chronic Internal Stressors

Internal stressors can be physically based, as in the case of infections, inflammation, chronic pain and other illness or disease.

They can also be due to our beliefs, feelings and thoughts such as:

- Fears and or phobias
- Chronic negative thinking
- Repetitive thought patterns
- Our sense of control
- Low self-esteem
- Personality traits
- Inability to be assertive
- Perception
- Worrying about future events
- Unrealistic, perfectionist expectations

Chronic External Stressors

Of concern to unretired Boomers, is that our workplace may be a major source of external stressors and this is discussed further in Chapter 13. External stressors are commonly found in the life areas of work, family, social and environment and examples are listed following.

They include:

Work	Family
• Work and non-work imbalance • Excessive job demands • Job insecurity • Conflicts with teammates and supervisors • Unclear job duties • Low pay • Understaffing • Bullying, Harassment • Workaholic • Urgent deadlines • Unreasonable workload • Making presentations in front of colleagues or clients • Unproductive and time-consuming meetings • Commuting and travel schedules • Unemployment • Excess working hours	• Conflict in family relationships • Persistent financial worries • Long term relationship problems • Empty nest syndrome • Having to care for a relative long term **Social** • Lack of social support or network • Difficult neighbors • Racism, Sexism • Poverty • Loneliness **Environment** • Excessive noise • Pollution • Traffic congestion • Inadequate housing

How we handle our stress load will determine the risk to our health. With unmanaged chronic stressors, we may experience varying degrees of illness that could lead to a life-threatening disease or even premature death.

For the remainder of this chapter, let's find out where you stand and explore strategies for managing the big **S.**

The Chronic Stress Symptom Inventory

Now is an opportune time to complete the *Chronic Stress Symptom Inventory* in **Appendix B.**

If your scores on the inventory are high, consult with your family doctor first, to rule out another medical reason for any symptoms or signs you're experiencing. If stressors are the culprit, then a stress management plan is required. This includes your doctor initially, but the daily actions to manage your plan are up to you and your support squad. It requires self-responsibility and taking charge, which is one of the keys to choosing and practicing a wellness lifestyle.

If you scored low on the Chronic Stress Symptom Inventory, continue to read through this chapter to learn more about the field of stress. It can serve as a reference should you ever find yourself in a chronically stressed state!

Stress management in a nutshell, is covered further on in this chapter.

Self-awareness and Resilience

The impact of unmanaged stressors in our lives puts us at risk for a health shock. Particularly significant are the thoughts, feelings and attitudes that make us our own worst enemies.

Many of us may be "flying under the radar" and not aware we are living chronically stressed. The most disturbing part of this is that over time our brain accepts this as the new normal and the cycle becomes self-perpetuating.

This can be reflected by our attitudes, beliefs and unhealthy habits. An example would be living with chronic stressors and *accepting* that it is *just* how things are in your work and/or home life. Another scenario is blaming your stressful state on external sources such as other people or events and believing you are powerless to make changes.

When we become aware of the chronic stressors in our lives, and take steps to minimize their impact, we regain a sense of control. This is not to say that any adversity we encounter in our lives is *pleasant* to experience, but we will cope better as we move through it.

Our capacity to weather the stressors in our lives is known as **resilience** which is derived from the Latin word "resilio" meaning to spring back or rebound.

A post from *Psychology Today* informs us that: "Resilience is that ineffable quality that allows some people to be knocked down by life and come back stronger than ever. Rather than letting failure overcome them and drain their resolve, they find a way to rise from the ashes. Psychologists have identified some of the factors that make someone resilient, among them a positive attitude, optimism, the ability to regulate emotions, and the ability to see failure as a form of helpful feedback. Even after a misfortune, resilient people are blessed with such an outlook that they are able to change course and soldier on."[11]

Resiliency is directly connected to wellbeing and relates to our ability to cope with and adapt to change and in doing so, adjust our balance. It can also be learned and developed over time and is not something we are born with or without.

Mindfully practicing **THE 4 FOUNDATIONAL LIFESTYLE HABITS** will bolster your resiliency.

Stress Management in a Nutshell

This section covers the basics of stress management and a more detailed approach will be tailored to an individual's needs in **A Complete Life Wellness Plan**™

The *first step* in stress management is assuming the attitude you are going to take charge of your life. This is best accomplished with the support of others, as we learn to become a change agent in our own lives.

In the *second step* write a list of the 10 main stressors (or more/ less) you are presently living with. You can use your results from the chronic stress inventory or the examples provided on the preceding pages, if required.

From here take each source of stress and find a strategy to delete and/or minimize them. This is the *third step* which takes planning, perseverance, support and a bit of courage, *but what is the alternative?*

In the remainder of this chapter we look at strategies that will guide you to take charge and manage your list.

I would buy a journal for stress management to keep track of your goals, actions, hurdles and successes. Date the page each time you enter new material to read again later, as a means of tracking what changes have taken place.

It can be tricky to determine if a stressor is external or internal or a mix as in the case of concluding that business meetings always "stress you out" when in reality better preparation would help minimize anxious feelings. I am speaking from personal experience!

Being aware, mindful of your thoughts, feelings and actions, put us in a better position to determine what the problem is and how best to deal with it.

Remember the Transactional Model that states: "It's our own internal beliefs, attitudes, interpretations, perceptions and other factors, in combination with the external events that tend to create stress."[12]

With a stress response, whether acute or chronic, the goal is to downgrade to a relaxation response. With this, our mind-body goes from fight or flight to a state of equilibrium or balance.

Next, let's look at some specific coping strategies for external and internal stressors.

Strategies for coping with external stressors

Techniques such as problem solving, time management, and decision-making are quick and simple to learn and essential for managing work and non-work stressors.

Improving communication skills with conflict resolution or assertiveness training, will give you greater control in expressing your needs, or negotiating with others to improve work and personal relationships. These **soft** skills can be developed over time, and are effective at managing a range of external stressors.

Strategies for coping with internal stressors

The severity of the internal stressors present will determine whether learning strategies to reframe your thoughts, challenge thinking traps, accept and constructively express emotions and/or working with a health professional is necessary. Generally, it is a good idea to speak with someone as we may be unaware of our own thinking and feeling patterns. Even one or two sessions with a professional can increase our self-awareness and assist us in developing strategies to reduce the effect of internal stressors!

Self-care and pampering is critical for stress management

It is important to take part in activities that are nurturing, relaxing and fun. Examples of these include:

- Learning and practicing mindfulness techniques to live more in the present
- Finding time for massage or sitting in a steam room or sauna
- Remembering to do abdominal breathing exercises (foundational lifestyle habit number four)
- Practicing yoga is great for improving our mind-body balance, especially for those sedentary unretired Boomers!
- Learning meditation to include as a daily practice
- Participating in fun activities like dancing
- Staying in touch with your sense of humour and feeling gratitude for your life

Lastly, in stress management some stressors can be eliminated, others you will need to accept (serenity prayer) and for the remainder you will need to change the situation or yourself or a combination of both to manage.

There is no manual for our lives, but choosing to practice a wellness lifestyle is an excellent substitute!

I hope this chapter has simplified the confusing world of stress and inspired you to look into it more closely.

The next chapter on the Intellectual dimension, supports that lifelong learning and applying **THE 4 FOUNDATIONAL LIFESTYLE HABITS** may decrease the odds of being diagnosed with dementia as we age.

There are other reasons to cultivate wellness in this dimension, as you will see in what follows.

INTELLECTUAL WELLNESS

Chapter Eight

Reality exists in the human mind, and nowhere else.
George Orwell, *1984*

When George Bernard Shaw published *Farfetched Fables* at 93, he was 30 years older than my present age. How is that for inspiration?

It's over when it's over I guess...

The following is a list of men and women in their 80's and 90's (except for Grandpa Moses) from *The Encyclopedia of Aging & The Elderly*[1] that shows what they were up to at the ages listed:

At Age

100   Grandma Moses was painting.

93   George Bernard Shaw wrote the play *Farfetched Fables*.

91   Eamon de Valera served as president of Ireland.

90   Pablo Picasso was producing drawings and engravings.

88   Michelangelo did architectural plans for the church of Santa Maria degli Angeli.

85   Coco Chanel was the head of a fashion design firm.

84   Somerset Maugham wrote *Points of View*.

82   Winston Churchill wrote a *History of English Speaking People*.

81 Johann Wolfgang von Goethe finished *Faust.*

80 George Bums won an Academy Award for his performance in *The Sunshine Boys*

There are many more people in their 60's – 70's and older who are working towards their goals and dreams or have realized them, that could be included. One of the qualities these unretired folks have in common is that their brains and intellect remain healthy into their advanced years.

WHAT IS INTELLECTUAL WELLNESS?

Intellectual wellness involves engaging in creative and stimulating activities that help us grow in this dimension. Improving our ability to think critically and share what we have learned with others is another part. This requires us to be curious and lifelong learners as previously mentioned. On this note, I may be curious to a fault!

Often the word intellectual is understood as referring to the academic world only, but it can relate to a variety of activities depending on the interests of a particular individual. Educational television programs, visiting museums or cultural events, staying current on local and global events, attending seminars or short continuing education courses are a few possibilities. Challenging our mind with crossword puzzles, or board games like chess, or math problems are other examples.

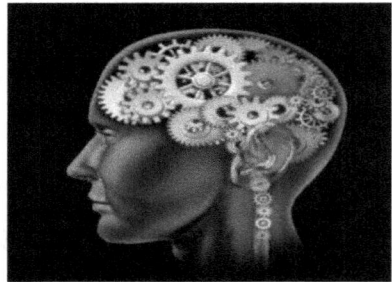

I find it exciting travelling to new cultures and exploring how they differ from the one I was raised in. Travelling is an example of one of my personal interests that stimulates my intellectual dimension.

Increasing our wellness in this dimension involves expanding our knowledge, acquiring new skills and remaining open to different ideas. In researching and writing this book I have learned new concepts, grappled with new facts and tapped into my creative ability. It is my experience and belief that the act of creating, whether it is through knitting, woodwork, writing, playing a musical instrument, painting, photography or other pursuits increases our wellbeing.

For unretired Boomers (or anyone really) if a creative activity is not part of how you spend your time, I recommend finding one that you like to do. This could become a goal in A Complete Life Wellness Plan™.

INITIATIVES TO KEEP THE BRAIN SHARP

There are organizations such as Lumosity (www.lumosity.com) which is an online brain training and neuroscience research company that: "offers a brain training program consisting of more than 40 games in the areas of memory, attention, flexibility, speed of processing, and problem solving."[2]

These games are available to the public as an online tool to exercise the intellectual dimension. This is definitely a step in the right direction and it will be exciting to see what unfolds with this creative company and others in this field.

As our intellectual dimension is "exercised "a cognitive reserve is thought to be developed and this is defined as "the brain's ability to operate effectively even when some function is disrupted or the amount of damage that the brain can sustain before changes in cognition are evident."[3]

By continuing to use and stretch our intellectual or cognitive capacity, our problem-solving and decision-making abilities improve.

THE IMPORTANCE OF THINKING STRAIGHT

As older workers that need to stay employed, taking steps to remain intellectually fit is advised. This is necessary to remain competitive in the labor market, let alone enjoy our life outside of working. In combination with exercising our intellect, looking after our brain's health by practicing **THE FOUR FOUNDATIONAL LIFESTYLE HABITS** may prevent, or delay the onset of dementia. A common cause of decline in cognition or intellectual function are diseases that cause dementia.

In North America (and globally) with the aging population, the number of persons living with dementia symptoms is becoming more apparent. A range of lives are touched by this disease whether it involves our spouse, parent(s), other family member, colleague or friend. It is a difficult situation many of us have to adjust to as somebody you once connected with or had a shared history develops dementia.

My mother, who I think about as I write these words, was recently diagnosed with dementia. She is in her early 90's and at the beginning stages. She was always regarded as possessing a sharp mind and wit, was a knitter, avid reader and put together complex jigsaw puzzles for many years, which may have delayed the onset of symptoms. There is a sense of loss and sadness I feel that accompanies these changes in her health. This experience has opened my eyes to a part of our world that is largely hidden away in long term care facilities, hospitals and private homes.

EXACTLY WHAT IS DEMENTIA?

A definition of dementia that is posted on the Alzheimer's Foundation of America website: "Dementia is a general term that describes a group of symptoms-such as loss of memory, judgment, language, complex motor skills, and other intellectual function-caused by the permanent damage or death of the brain's nerve cells, or neurons."

One or more of several diseases, including Alzheimer's, can cause dementia.

Alzheimer's disease is the most common cause of dementia in persons over the age of 65. It represents about 60 percent of all dementias.

"The other most common causes of dementia are vascular dementia, caused by stroke or blockage of blood supply, and dementia with Lewy bodies. Other types include alcohol dementia, caused by sustained use of alcohol; trauma dementia, caused by head injury; and a rare form of dementia, frontotemporal dementia." [4]

AT WHAT AGE DOES IT OCCUR?

There has been a significant amount of interest and research performed on the brain in recent years. A large part of this has been in response to the incidence of dementia and related diseases of the mind worldwide. It is stated in a report titled *Rising Tide: The Impact of Dementia on Canadian Society* in regards to dementia that: " It is the most significant cause of disability among Canadians (65+) and it already costs Canadian society many billions of dollars each year."[5]

The following statistics are revealing and provide an incentive to take preventative actions.

The Alzheimer Society of Canada reports that: "Between 2 per cent and 10 per cent of all cases of dementia start before the age of 65.4. The risk for dementia doubles every five years after age 65.4"[6]

I present this information not to depress anyone but to increase awareness and also show the value of a choosing and practicing a wellness lifestyle.

What can be done in the name of prevention for these diseases of the brain/mind/body? In the next section, the four foundational habits are brought forward to address this question, along with one of my favourite topics, stress management!

THE 4 FOUNDATIONAL LIFESTYLE HABITS

The brain is one of the body's key organs. It is often overlooked, yet is the seat of our mind and navigation system.

Here are **THE 4 FOUNDATIONAL LIFESTYLE HABITS** mentioned in Chapter 6, with a brief summary of the health benefits, each habit offers our brain/mind/body.

1) **Regular physical exercise** may lower blood pressure and cholesterol or help prevent a diagnosis of diabetes and these are all risk factors for dementia. Physical exercise is essential in managing stress. Research indicates that exercise is also involved in the production of new nerve cells and minute

blood vessels in the brain. All of these benefits are good for the heart and brain and major reasons to "just do it."

2) **A nutritional diet** that results in stable blood sugar levels will help prevent the onset of diabetes. Diet, keeping our weight down and exercise together will work towards maintaining acceptable levels of good and bad cholesterol. Spending time with a nutritionist or researching online to put together healthy meal plans and learn about eating right (brain foods) will be a solid investment of your time.

3) The importance of our **sleeping well** is mentioned in Chapter 6 where the Division of Sleep Medicine at Harvard Medical School advises that: "insufficient sleep increases a person's risk of developing serious medical conditions, including obesity, diabetes, and cardiovascular disease."[7]

4) Abdominal or **diaphragmatic breathing** can be easily learned and practiced as an ongoing habit to ensure that our brain and body are receiving sufficient oxygen-rich blood and removing cellular waste. It is also an important and effective technique for managing stress.

Stressors and Brain Health

Unmanaged chronic stressors can speed up the aging process and involve increased exposure to several of the risk factors related to dementia. Staying engaged with and supported by our family, friends and others in our networks and community plays a significant role in offsetting the effect of stressors and/ or staying intellectually fit. The social dimension is looked at in more detail in Chapter 10.

In another excerpt from *Rising Tide: The Impact of Dementia on Canadian Society* it is stated that: "The accepted view today is that promoting brain health through **lifestyle choices is the most effective way** of reducing the chances of developing Alzheimer's disease or a related dementia or slowing down the progression of these diseases in people who already have them. Adopting a lifestyle that ignores risk factors does not mean, however, that one will develop the disease, but it does increase the odds."[8]

It is apparent from the information above, that the wellness dimensions are inter-connected and choosing and practicing a wellness lifestyle will contribute to our brain and body health and capacity for intellectual fitness, as we age.

The next chapter presents the Spiritual dimension, another important concept that is often misunderstood. Our spiritual wellness, like the other dimensions make up part of our total health.

Have you had any eureka-like experiences regarding your holistic nature? If not, it should become more evident as you continue to read through the remaining chapters/dimensions of **The Un-Retirement Guide™**!

SPIRITUAL WELLNESS

Chapter Nine

What each of us believes in is up to us, but life is
impossible without believing in something
Kentetsu Takamori

Why is spirituality important? Do you agree that there are "truths" in all faiths?

I grew up in a large family, that among other things were practicing Catholics. We were taught that the Holy Spirit or Holy Ghost guided the Catholic Church by sharing God's word through sacred tradition and scripture.

The word spirit has numerous definitions and: "comes from the Latin spiritus, meaning "breath," but also spirit, soul, courage, vigor."[1] By extension, spiritual applies to that which consists of the soul or spirit as opposed to our physical body or nature.

As a boy, I found the Catholic Mass and theology complex and difficult to comprehend. I did enjoy the fellowship, including that our family was usually together for mass. None of us liked missing breakfast though in order to fast for Holy Communion which was received later during the Sunday service. By the time we got home for a late meal everyone was ravenous!

These days, I no longer attend a church regularly, but keep an open mind about those who do and I believe in the power of prayer.

What comes to your mind when you see or hear the word "spiritual"? A common answer is that it refers to religion or religious beliefs.

Everyone has a spiritual component, but not everyone is religious. A comparison of the two is provided by the Merck Manual: "Religion and spirituality are similar but not identical concepts. Religion is often viewed as more institutionally based, more structured, and more traditional and may be associated with organized, well-established beliefs. Spirituality refers to the intangible and immaterial and thus may be considered a more general term, not associated with a particular group or organization. It can refer to feelings, thoughts, experiences, and behaviors related to the soul or to a search for the sacred (e.g., a Divine Being, Ultimate Reality, Ultimate Truth)."[2]

The spiritual need for connection with the divine may be fulfilled in a community church, temple, mosque or other gathering place or a personal relationship with a higher power and may involve prayer, singing, meditation, chanting, fellowship, being alone or other. The main stipulation is that however you accomplish this; it does not harm yourself or others.

The next sections will look closer at connection and meaning, the two parts that make up spiritual wellness.

Connection

A definition of Spirituality provided by the University of Minnesota website states: "Spirituality is a broad concept with room for many perspectives. In general, it includes a sense of connection to something bigger than ourselves, and typically involves a search for meaning in life. As such, it is a universal human experience— something that touches us all. People may describe a spiritual experience as sacred or transcendent or simply a deep sense of aliveness and interconnectedness."[3]

Spiritual wellness then relates to: developing a personal sense of connection to God and/or a power greater than ourselves and creating meaning in our lives.

Positive inner states of peace, gratitude and hope are indicators that your efforts to find connection and meaning are succeeding.

Meaning

The second part of spiritual wellness is how we seek and express meaning in our lives. This will differ for each person and change over time as our circumstances do.

Examples of how meaning can be experienced include but are not limited to:

- Religious or personal beliefs and practices that aim at connecting us to God or a higher power.
- Meaningful connection may also be found by spending time in nature, listening to music, artistic pursuits or other activities.

- Relationships with others can give our lives meaning.
- Meaning and direction may be experienced when our individual purpose is clarified and our daily intention, choices and actions are based upon this. Living on purpose will help develop integrity and fulfill our spiritual needs.

Purpose

"What is your purpose?" is a new age question that is often asked these days and with it comes the notion that it is difficult to define and might require changing the world! For some, changing the lives of others on a large scale may be their life purpose, but for many it will be closer to home and this does take away from its importance or the spiritual benefit.

Our individual purposes will vary. My mother's revolved around her family, for others it may be their work, or how they practice their faith or a combination of things. What matters is that our purpose is realized and acted upon in whatever form it takes. This gives our life meaning and direction.

Since ancient times the: "Native Americans follow their ancestors' two purposes of life: to know the self and be of help to others. They vest many of their beliefs and spiritual powers in nature, the land, and animals." [4] This provided the connection to something larger and is very different from the beliefs of Christianity or other forms of religion. These differences if accepted, are an example of diversity and inclusion within free societies.

The two purposes mentioned above; know the self and be of help to others, combine to underline what authentic purpose is. To move from a self-centered purpose to one that is focussed on service to others places us on the spiritual path. What we are talking about in essence, is loving ourselves and others.

Purpose, like wellness, exists on a continuum and is something we grow into where the ultimate goal is to know the self (live with integrity) and be of service to others. I'm sure many Boomers live in this manner or are evolving in this direction. It is good to review the information provided in this chapter (and others) though, as many of us may be pre-occupied with reaching our financial goals.

A good place to start, and come back to as our lives change, is reflecting on the big picture questions. Examples of a few questions that I have pondered are listed below. I provided a sample of my answers to illustrate.

Why am I alive?

- Learn to accept myself unconditionally
- Have fun and laugh often
- Cherish each moment and not squander my time while alive
- Grow into my potential and create along the way
- Do the best I can each day
- Practice building bridges to others and helping out if needed

What do I find fulfilling in my life?

- Spending time with family and friends
- Living a wellness lifestyle
- Belonging to a spiritual community that provides connection
- Travelling and experiencing, embracing diversity

Where do I fit in?

- With others who are adventurous and into exploring their potential

- In the helping professions

- As part of the wellness community

Each person may have different answers depending on their spiritual perspective; there are no right or wrong responses. Answers to these or other life purpose questions can ground us and provide a spiritual foundation to build connection, meaning, and purpose upon.

A purpose in life is a feeling of wellbeing that comes from having meaning and direction and knowing that what you do is needed and matters. This is turn will provide guidance and strength along the way.

Work can provide purpose and meaning, and this is especially true if your strengths, interests and values are aligned to how you earn money. Taking the self-assessment in Chapter 16 is a great starting point to assist in identifying your strengths, interests and values, which will further breakdown your life purpose. I encourage you to check this and other sources out.

Developing spiritual wellness involves setting our intention and making choices and actions that fulfill our need for connection and meaning. Like other aspects of wellness this is an opportunity for growth to occur and can become a goal in A Complete Life Wellness Plan™.

Health, Longevity and Spiritual Wellness

There are many studies that correlate connection and meaning with health and longevity, an example of these findings follow.

"Medicine has begun to recognize the strong influence of spirituality on health and illness. Studies of cancer patients have shown that those who continuously pursue goals related to living a meaningful life boost the natural killer cell activity in their immune systems."[5]

"Gerontology professionals agree that spirituality is important to older adults towards effective psychosocial function and successful aging."[6]

To summarize then, the Spiritual dimension is another aspect of our health that influences our quality of life, including the ability to stay employed as unretired Boomers, and is an important part of a wellness lifestyle.

The next chapter, on the social dimension examines in part, the fact that we are hardwired to be social creatures! Amy Banks, M.D., director of Advanced Training at the Jean Baker Miller Training Institute states that: "Due to a series of seminal studies and research, neuroscience is confirming our entire autonomic nervous system wants us to connect with other human beings."[7]

Please join me in the pages that follow to look at what the ingredients of social wellness are, and how it adds to our wholeness.

SOCIAL WELLNESS

Chapter Ten

*Social progress can be measured by the social
position of the female sex.*
Karl Marx

Human beings are social creatures, and as such wellness in this
dimension has a significant bearing on our quality of life.

It appears that children have been granted special powers that
foster bonding with their parents, grandparents or caregivers. The
family bond is a strong force which is in most cases mutually
beneficial and lends to the survival of the human species.

The initial bond or connection we have with our caregivers is an
important template that we will use in our adult relationships to
meet our social needs. For the most part, humans are nurtured to
varying degrees in childhood. I believe that we can learn how to
create more social connection and support in our lives if need be,
and will discuss this later.

Most of us have experienced social wellbeing in our lives and quite
possibly still do. How do you describe what this looks or feels like in
your life? Most likely it involves people we like, or love that support
us. Another aspect is a shared history and acceptance of each other
through thick or thin.

Social interactions can be unpleasant and unpredictable also. Examples of this are a heated disagreement with a family member or
friend, or the unprovoked rudeness of a stranger.

The Need to Connect

I spent two years in the prairie province of Manitoba, living in a small community called St. Norbert. There would be periodic public "socials" which were gatherings at the local community hall where dancing and mingling took place. Part of the reasoning for these events was to break up the long, cold winters and the need to recreate and connect. Many of those attending were locals and knew of each other.

Social connection can create meaning and purpose in our life. Another way to describe this is that it reduces the sense of feeling lonely or isolated. As I write these words, I am in Krabi, Thailand. At times I feel disconnected because I do not speak the language, so I'm not able to communicate with the Thais, let alone experience a connection. If I was to live here part of the year, as I am considering doing, I would take language lessons and also seek out the English-speaking expat community to cultivate a social network. A certain amount of solitude is healthy, but we need to develop a balance between being alone and spending time with others.

An article on social wellness from *The Center for Aging with Dignity* (2008, 2011) advises that: "researchers recommend these questions to differentiate between an isolated person and those who are not isolated:

- Who is the one special person you could call or contact if you needed help?
- In general, rather than your children, how many relatives do you feel close to and have contact with at least once a month?
- In general, how many friends do you feel close to?"[1]

If your answers to these questions indicate you have few people to confide in or who "have your back", then you may be socially isolated. Part of a wellness lifestyle could involve taking steps to increase the number of supportive people in your life. I have been told you should have at least one person outside of family member(s) that you can confide in or who accept you as you are, a lifeline so to speak. Obviously more than one friend is desirable but quality is better than quantity.

It may also be necessary to end relationships if they are toxic to your wellbeing.

Lastly, on this note, it took me a long time to get to the point where I felt inner peace while alone. I attribute this personal development in part, to the practice of meditation and surrendering to a higher power.

Atul Gawande an American surgeon and author comments on our need for others by stating: "Human beings are social creatures. We are social not just in the trivial sense that we like company, and not just in the obvious sense that we each depend on others. We are social in a more elemental way: simply to exist as a normal human being requires interaction with other people."[2]

On a deeper level, research in the field of: "Neuroscience has discovered that our brain's very design makes it sociable, inexorably drawn into an intimate brain-to-brain linkup whenever we engage with another person. That neural bridge lets us impact the brain — and so the body—of everyone we interact with, just as they do us."[3]

In addition to our basic survival it is through each other that we create and define who we are. We may be more like a school of fish or flock of birds that move simultaneously than we are aware of!

Amy Banks, M.D., author and instructor of Psychiatry at Harvard Medical School takes this further, stating: "Due to a series of seminal studies and research, neuroscience is confirming our entire autonomic nervous system wants us to connect with other human beings. Of particular importance are mirror neurons, which are throughout our brain and allow us to read behavior. There have been studies that look at emotions in human beings such as disgust, shame, happiness, where the exact same areas of the brain light up in the listener who is reading the feelings of the person talking. We are literally, hardwired to connect. Our greatest gift is to connect, and we function better in connection as individuals and as a society." [4]

I'm still writing these words from Krabi, Thailand. It is apparent as I circulate in this community that the Thais are gregarious and value social connection, and this has been reinforced by the use of cell phone technology!

Communicating our Needs

In order to enhance our social wellness, we need the ability to clearly communicate with ourselves and others. Sharpening my communication skills is an ongoing step for me in my wellness plan.

All the wellness dimensions may be involved in communication! A working definition found on Chase Fleming's excellent com-munication studies website advises that; "The act of communicating draws on several interpersonal and intrapersonal skills. These include speaking, listening, observing, questioning, processing, analysing and evaluating. Recipients of a message must be able to identify the sender's intent, take into account the message's context, resolve any misunderstandings, accurately decode the information and decide how to act on it."[5]

Quite remarkably, we are able to communicate with each other in spite of how complex the process is. "It's estimated that up to 7,000 different languages are spoken around the world and 90% of these languages are used by less than 100,000 people."[6]

Communication can be verbal and/or non-verbal. It has been found that: "In recent years, a wave of studies has documented some incredible emotional and physical health benefits that come from touch. This research is suggesting that touch is truly fundamental to human communication, bonding, and health."[7]

Touch can be communicated in the form of friendly hugging, a handshake or pat on the back, sexually, a massage or other body-work.

Intimacy Outside of Sex

If our efforts to communicate and connect are successful, the resulting reward of intimacy may be experienced. This is not always our intention, but in interactions where it is: "Intimacy generally refers to the feeling of being in a close personal association and belonging together. It is a familiar and very close affective con-nection with another as a result of a bond that is formed through knowledge and experience of the other."[8]

There are other sources of intimacy other than one that is sexual in nature which is what is commonly associated with this term. Intimacy can also be experienced from a shared emotional, intellectual, recreational, work or spiritual connection. *The more of these experienced, the greater we are accurately seen, reflected and understood.* This results in decreased self-consciousness and increased self-acceptance when we are in each other's company. Or to put it another way we become more at home in our own skin.

The wisdom of divine planning is evident here with our innate potential for connection and intimacy!

What does social wellness look like?

Part of our shared humanity is that we make mistakes socially and otherwise. This is allowable and encouraged and takes a degree of courage, if we choose to grow in this dimension.

I draw a line in the sand for what I consider unacceptable behaviour from others, while at the same time practicing compassion and remaining open to our differences. I shy away from negativity or abusive individuals and categorize them under "Toxic." It does not mean I would not help them in dire circumstances, but I am selective in who I want to share my nervous system with!

The bulleted points below are high level definitions of social wellness and the direction to work towards.

Indicators of social wellness:

1. Can be time spent with others that is educational, inspiring, entertaining, fun and filled with laughter—yah!
2. Live and work independently, yet maintains satisfying relationships with others.
3. Value solitude and our own company at times, to reflect and recharge.
4. Creates a support system that includes family members and friends.
5. Is the ability to positively interact with people in your work and non-work life.
6. Develops good communications skills to ask for what you need and be responsive to the needs of others.
7. Manages any conflict that arises with the intent to build bridges rather than burn them.
8. Is your willingness to give and receive help in the community you live in.

9. Accepts human diversity whether it is in the form of age, size, religion, gender, sexual orientation, ability or race with the intention of living in harmony.

Mind-Body Benefits of Social Wellness

Social isolation involves a lack of connection, intimacy and may be due to the nature of our modern lifestyles and/or the inability to communicate and fulfill our social needs which are: "things such as acceptance, appreciation, belonging and companionship. Essentially, social needs are met by forging relationships with other people. Social needs are most often discussed in reference to Maslow's Hierarchy of Needs."[9]

The psychologist Abraham Maslow's Hierarchy of Human Needs, is one of the most widely used theories of motivation. The hierarchy is often portrayed as a pyramid, with the most basic needs at the bottom and the more complex ones at the top. It was proposed by Dr. Maslow that the lower needs (social) require fulfilling before being able to move onto higher needs, such as growing as an individual and/or fulfilling our potential. As with most theories, there are a few psychologists who aren't in total agreement with Dr. Maslow.

Research on why Social Wellness is important

The Public Health Agency of Canada (2013) reports suggests: "Some experts in the field have concluded that the health effect of social relationships may be as important as established risk factors such as smoking, physical activity, obesity and high blood pressure. An extensive study in California found that, for men and women, the more social contacts people have, the lower their premature death rates. Another U.S. study found that low availability of emotional support and low social participation was associated with all-cause mortality. The risk of angina pectoris decreased with increasing levels of emotional support in a study of male Israeli civil servants."[10]

The findings from the studies above, add social isolation as another risk factor towards a shortened lifespan and increased incidence of cardiovascular disease. Additional research points to the following health benefits that are the result of a supportive social network such as: the buffering of stressors which assists in relaxing a stress response, lowered risk of depression, memory loss and better adjustment to the unfolding of old age.

Does this mean we have to run out and drum up a large support network or else we will succumb to illness and or disease? **No**, but developing social wellness will contribute to work, family and personal success and enhance our overall life satisfaction.

The people in our environments are important, and so is the environment itself, as explored in the next chapter.

Environmental Wellness

Chapter Eleven

The environment is everything that isn't me.
Albert Einstein

The environmental dimension is often overlooked in wellness planning. Choosing and practicing a wellness lifestyle involves all seven dimensions, including the environmental.

Our primary environment is internal (mind-body) as we live, work, learn, rest and recreate in multiple external environments. These include but are not limited to our residence, workplace and community, expanding outwards to the planet we inhabit.

Improving our wellness involves becoming more aware of the related issues and/or matters that affect our daily lives in a particular dimension.

Doing the best we can to make informed choices about the environmental actions we take, will move us towards increased wellness in this dimension.

As a global citizen: "Environmental wellbeing involves being aware of the limits of the earth's natural resources, and understanding the impact of your actions on the environment. Environmentally well people consciously choose to live in ways that protect the world around them. Being environmentally well enhances your personal health, and helps ensure the future health of our communities and the world."[1]

97

Examples of what activities and attitudes add to our balance in this dimension are provided next.

Indicators of Environmental Wellness

- People that are environmentally well:
- Spend time recreating outside in natural settings.
- Cherish and volunteer in any manner to promote living in a safe and clean community and the availability of healthy food, air and water.
- Compost and recycle plastic, paper, cans and glass as best they can.
- Question the necessity of everything they consume and how it might be used and or disposed of.
- Conserve electrical energy and limit idling their vehicle engine and unnecessary use. Walking and bicycling are great alternatives to driving.
- This was mentioned in Chapter 4, but due to its importance I will do so again: take measures for protection from environmental hazards including, safety issues, toxic chemicals, air and water pollution, harmful solar radiation, second-hand smoke and noise.
- Create personal and work spaces that are safe, ergonomic and maintained, promote a greater sense of balance or harmony.

Our personal responsibility to minimize any environmental footprint we may leave, doesn't stop or become any less important as we age.

Environmental wellness can be enhanced by access to community facilities such as nature parks, theaters, libraries, pools and town squares that promote leisure, entertainment and/or relaxation.

In the community where I live, there are also many environmental initiatives underway that could be fun to participate in.

Moving on

As I write these words from Krabi, Thailand on their New Year's Day, April 13, 2015, I wish my readers well-being and prosperity for the years ahead.

The next chapter on the occupational dimension is the last of the seven dimensions discussed, but certainly not the least.

OCCUPATIONAL WELLNESS

Chapter Twelve

It is better to fail in originality than to succeed in imitation.
Herman Melville

Occupational in The Un-Retirement Guide™ refers to the work we do as employees or self-employed persons, to make a living. The occupational dimension is one of seven that make up
A Complete Life Wellness Plan™.

Due to its importance for unretired Boomers, a five part (Chapters 13-17) occupational series that follows in **Part 3** was included to guide older workers towards increasing their balance in the occupational dimension.

Indicators of occupational wellness listed below touch on purpose, manageable stressors, the opportunity for growth and other conditions. There is also the important indicator of adequate compensation and benefits, the basis of building wealth.

For unretired Boomers (and everyone else), financial freedom is a sought after goal. If we have enough income from a financial portfolio to pay our essential expenses only, we could consider ourselves free from working, but our standard of living would be limited. For me, the amount of wealth I am trying to accumulate would allow for a comfortable and sustainable standard of living that would cover essential and certain leisure expenses such as travel.

According to Rich Dad's Robert Kiyosaki: "The definition of wealth is the number of days you can survive without physically working (or anyone in your household physically working) and still maintain your standard of living. For example, if your monthly expenses are $5,000 and you have $20,000 in savings, your wealth is approximately four months or 120 days. Wealth is measured in time, not dollars."[1]

Or if your monthly expenses were $1,000 per month your wealth would be 20 months. What Mr. Kiyosaki states is interesting, and if you think about it, profound.

Meaning and Purpose in our work

Performing work that is aligned with who we are as individuals is the preferred route to accumulating wealth. If our employment is aligned with our strengths, values, and interests our sense of meaning and purpose is deepened.

It may take years to find our niche occupationally and require taking courses, changing jobs and increasing our self-awareness around what we like to do and have to offer.

Maybe you started out in a well-defined career path as a young adult and continued on it your entire working life. I wasn't one of these individuals and had a number of false starts until identifying and upgrading into my niche in the field of career and rehabilitation counselling. I once had a survival job *shovelling steel ball bearings* at a cement plant!

The next section lists some indicators of high level occupational wellness to aim for, if you are not already there. See what other dimensions (emotional, physical, intellectual etc.) you can identify in each indicator.

Indicators of High Level Occupational Wellness

- There is a connection between your strengths, values, interests and job tasks and responsibilities

- Finds their job interesting and it provides personal satisfaction.

- Has adequate amount of control over the workload and environment.

- Is able to meet the demands of family and work responsibilities and has personal time for oneself (Chapter 13).

- Able to cope with workplace stressors through a plan of action.

- Developing the ability to build collaborative relationships with co-workers.

- The compensation and benefits are sufficient to meet present financial needs and contribute towards building wealth.

- There is opportunity for career development through sponsored or cost-shared work related training.

- There are safety policies and practices in place and supportive ergonomics such as proper lighting and individually designed work stations.

The indicators of occupational wellness listed above are an ideal we aim towards.

Part 3 which is next, contains five chapters (13-17) written for older workers who are unemployed or under-employed, confronted with age discrimination, work stressed and/or struggling to stay gainfully employed.

Part 3
Staying Gainfully Employed and More

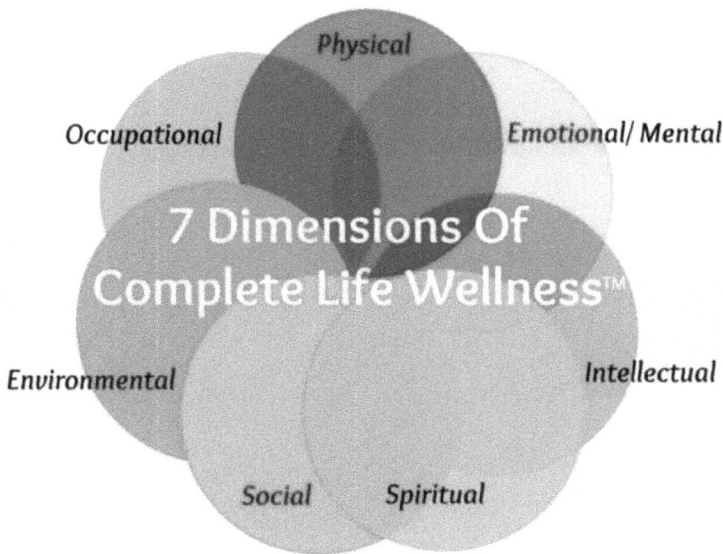

7 Dimensions Of Complete Life Wellness™

Physical
Occupational
Emotional/Mental
Environmental
Intellectual
Social
Spiritual

WORK STRESSORS AND MENTAL HEALTH

Chapter Thirteen

There is no work-life balance. We have one life.
What's most important is that you be awake for it.
Janice Marturano

We looked at the topic of stress in chapter seven and will do so again in this chapter. What follows is more need to know information aimed at staying gainfully employed.

Keeping it Together

Mental health is the degree of how *well* we think, feel and behave. The World Health Organization (2014) states that: "Mental health is an integral part of health; indeed, there is no health without mental health. Mental health is a state of well-being in which every individual realizes his or her own potential, can cope with the normal *stresses* of life, can work productively and fruitfully, and is able to make a contribution to her or his community."[1]

The American Institute of Stress comments that "Numerous studies show that job stress is far and away the major source of stress for American adults and that it has escalated progressively over the past few decades.

Increased levels of job stress as assessed by the perception of having little control but lots of demands have been demonstrated to be associated with increased rates of heart attack, hypertension and other disorders."[2]

The Marchand-Durand study (2013) on mental health in the workplace found that: "Job insecurity, abusive supervision, excessive demands, the encroachment of work on family life and domestic relationship problems top the list of factors that contribute to the development of mental health issues among workers."[3]

Stressors involved in triggering mental illness can occur externally and/or internally. They can originate at work and during personal time and are often chronic. The Marchand-Durand study mentioned above found that one of the top contributing factors to mental distress was "the encroachment of work on family life." This relates to our attempts to find enough time for our personal needs as well as those of family, friends, community and work.

Older workers may not need to juggle raising children, as is the case with Millennials or Gen X, but could be stressed over attending to the needs of ailing partners/parents and adult children or grand-children.

If the stressors are unmanaged and chronic, our mind-body health is at risk. Employers and employees need to be aware of this and not just sweep it under the carpet.

Considering that job stressors pose serious health risks, the next section offers strategies to help employees cope.

What can employees do to manage job stress?

- Try to set boundaries (say no with a reason) around taking on additional work.

- Develop skills in assertive communication, time manage-ment, organization, planning and decision-making.

- Use the above skills to learn to negotiate, prioritize your work and delegate if able.

- Make a list of sources of stress related to work and outside of work and create a plan to minimize as described in Chapter 7.

- Discuss with an employer situations involving conflict or stress, such as being overloaded, which are affecting your mental health. Take and use your vacation days and other time off to build resilience.

- If you are experiencing chronic mental health symptoms such as feeling depressed, anxious, confused or unable to cope and cannot resolve this through talking with family and or friends, go and see a professional counsellor. Many employ-ers are connected to confidential Employee and Family Assistance Programs (EFAP).

In addition to the strategies above, certain workplaces provide disability management programs that include rehabilitation services for workers, as discussed below.

What can employers do?

- Implement a disability management plan that focuses on prevention, early intervention and return-to-work assistance for stress-related mental health claims. This will raise awareness of mental health issues in the workplace and the financial costs of ignoring them.

- Provide an online forum or suggestion box for employees to confidentially offer feedback on stressor hotspots. Other activities could be: in-house training to raise awareness of workplace stressors and reduce the stigma of mental illness; and the creation and/or enforcement of policies to prevent workplace discrimination, harassment and bullying.

- Include a Health and Wellness program that assists employees in creating and tracking an ongoing wellness lifestyle. The goal would be to develop positive mental health. Implementing such a program demonstrates management's commitment to establishing a healthy psychological workplace, where employees are supported.

Employer-based wellness programs and their benefits are supported by many Provincial and State jurisdictions. In British Columbia, for example the Ministry of Health writes that: "Organizational *wellness* initiatives focus on the working environment by changing or improving factors such as leadership style, management practices, the way in which work is organized, employee autonomy and control, and *social support*. These factors have been shown to have a dramatic impact on employee health outcomes. Workplaces that promote organizational *wellness* support both employee health and a strong bottom line, with reduced absenteeism, turnover, health and compensation costs."[4]

Fulfilling our Needs

Not getting our personal and family needs met generates stressful feelings, which in turn can lead to health issues.

Christine M. Riordan, (2013) professor of management at the University of Kentucky, advises: "Research has in fact shown that employees who believe they do not have time for their personal life feel drained and distracted while they are at work. In addition, the *spillover* of the negative aspect of work into an employee's personal life can lead to job exhaustion, disruption of relationships with family and friends, loss of enjoyment, and increased *stress*."[5]

Before moving on, I should point out that certain, but not all employers offer flexibility initiatives such as telecommuting, a compressed work week, home office days and other modifications aimed at reducing mental health issues for employees.

Other wellness initiatives for older employees include but are not limited to:

- on-site childcare programs for grandchildren if required;
- availability of eldercare resources to help with aging and or ailing parents;

- different types of leave policies including sabbaticals, parental, educational, mental health and family responsibility days;

- opportunities for personal development; and

- paid passes for fitness facilities.

In addition to these standard approaches, Personal Performance Consultants (2012) advise that: "Achieving good mental health requires a **holistic approach**. Mental well-being can be affected *by relationships with family, friends and coworkers, anger, sleep, financial issues, eating habits and physical activity – and many other factors in your work and other areas of life*. Successful action on one requires an understanding of how these factors are interconnected."[7]

Prioritizing our health through a wellness lifestyle.

Shepell fgi, who is the largest Canadian-based provider of Employment Family Assistance Program services, offers a solution: "These days, countless studies point to the need for balancing home and work life to reduce stress, and increase personal and professional satisfaction and effectiveness. One of the best ways to start balancing the demands on our time, talents and energy is to make our own health and wellness a priority. Making personal health a motivating factor in our daily decisions makes it easier to choose positive, strengthening actions over those that are negative, unnecessary or destructive."[6]

We are multi-dimensional beings where each of the seven dimensions of our life affects the other. There is no boundary between who we are, whether at or away from work. Assessing and adjusting those dimensions that are out of balance is the holistic approach to improving mind, body, spiritual health in the workplace.

The term work-life balance is limited when viewed from a wellness perspective and primarily concerns itself with time management and flexibility initiatives. These are useful tools though, to include in our career management and wherever else they may apply.

The next chapter brings up the potential barrier of age discrimination that older workers may encounter, along with strategies to overcome common stereotypes.

ı

HITTING IT HEAD ON – DEALING WITH AGEISM

Chapter Fourteen

The secret of staying young is to live honestly,
eat slowly, and lie about your age
Lucille Ball

As I sat across from Robert (alias) at the local Starbucks and listened to him tell me that "the new generation will never be able to take over the helm from Boomers because they have no work ethic" it occurred to me that his opinion was a stereotype. I asked him "How else is the younger generation different from us Robert?" and he replied, "With all the time spent on their cell phones, they will never learn how to properly communicate, if somebody wants to get a hold of me they can call my landline!" I asked Robert "Do you think technology could help us work smarter in a different way?" He said "When I was young, I was taught the value of a hard day's work and people talked to each other face to face, not on Facebook."

After getting home I reflected on our conversation as I was writing this chapter. Robert demonstrated the kind of inflexible attitude and beliefs that age stereotypes portray, an unwillingness to adapt to change.

In a separate social situation, I recently attended, a communication training course in conflict resolution. I was 20 plus years older than the other students who were professionals such as lawyers, middle and upper management, teachers, etc. We were required to role play *fun topics* like feeling vulnerable or to work in small teams to build objects with unusual materials that really couldn't be built, as we found out later! The course was three days long and during those days at times I felt that I was too old, not smart enough and did not belong. This was my perception and self-consciousness at work. It was the first time in my life where I became aware of being an "older student." I compared this to the type of feelings associated with being on the receiving end of age discrimination: not pleasant.

It also made me think about how we internalize these stereotypes from the culture we live in. I have caught myself making statements such as "When you get to be my age" or "When I was younger" and these types of comments need to be checked at the door.

Not only is age discrimination painful, it is unfair and can pose a barrier to finding or maintaining a job. It can also be experienced in settings other than the workplace.

For unretired Boomers who need, or wish to stay employed up to and past the age of 65, the incidence of ageism encountered may increase. This is due to long-held cultural beliefs and policies that we stop working at or before 65, because at this age we are too old to work. To be accurate, certain older individuals who have attitude issues discussed later in this chapter, may no longer be competitively employable.

Human Rights and Discrimination

Ageism is stereotyping and discriminating against individuals or groups on the basis of their age

The Ontario Human Rights Commission describes age discrimination in employment as: "Assumptions and stereo-types about older workers are unfortunately all too prevalent in our workplaces. Older workers are often unfairly perceived as less productive, less committed to their jobs, not dynamic or innovative, un-receptive to change, unable to be trained or costly to the organization due to health problems and higher salaries. These ideas about older workers are simply myths that are not borne out by evidence. In fact, there is significant evidence that older workers:

- are highly-productive, offering considerable on-the-job experience;
- do as well or better than younger workers on creativity, flexibility, information processing, accident rates, absenteeism and turnover;
- can learn as well as younger workers with appropriate training methods and environments; and
- do not fear change but rather fear discrimination."[1]

In the United States, employment-related age discrimination charges can be filed through the US Equal Employment Opportunity Commission. In Canada the governing body is the Canadian Human Rights Commission.

Effects of Ageism and its Practice in the Workforce

Jen Laskey (2008) provides the following definition of Ageism and the psychological effects. "Ageism refers to a basic denial of older people's human rights. The term was coined in 1968 by Robert N. Butler, M.D., a gerontologist, psychiatrist, and Pulitzer Prize–winning author. Like racism or sexism, ageism has a myriad of negative effects on emotional well-being. Age-based discrimination can decrease one's self-esteem; it can cause feelings of stress, anxiety, guilt, shame, or helplessness. Others may also be quick to accept stereotypes about aging, thus compounding these effects."[2]

Alison Doyle, a job search expert advises that "Employment discrimination happens when a job seeker or an employee is treated unfavorably because of his or her race, skin color, national origin, gender, disability, religion, or *age*."[3]

The next paragraph is of particular interest to unretired Boomers:

> How ageism is practiced is summarized by Kacey Stapleton (2009) in the following excerpt: "Ageism in the workplace is usually seen as a prejudice against anyone nearing or passing the standard age of retirement. Discrimination can either be systematic or incidental denial of employment, advancement or fair treatment. Systematic discrimination means an employer deliberately instructs management either against hiring individuals of a certain age or to force out workers as they near the age of retirement." [4]

Age discrimination can occur not only from a younger person towards an older one, but also in the other direction. Members of the older generation such as Robert may view younger workers as inexperienced, or not reliable to name a few additional stereotypes, and values can clash. These types of discrimination issues can be found in the increasing number of inter-generational workplaces.

Beliefs Underlying Ageism

A post retrieved from the Older Adults-Aging in Canada website (2012) indicates that: "Older adults in the workplace are often perceived to be lower in productivity, slower in decision making, resistant to change, and slow to learn. Evidence suggests that this is not the case. Even with radical changes in technology and the expectations of faster and more intensified work, older workers are as productive as their younger counterparts with the appropriate training."[5]

The central issue is not necessarily what your age is, but one of attitude of those perpetuating ageism. *Read the list of six common stereotypes below* and determine if they hold true for you. If so, then it will become part of your homework to address them as need be.

If stereotypes aren't a barrier for you, whether maintaining a job or searching for one, then you need to look at other aspects of your personal career profile (chapter 16).

Older Worker Stereotypes and Strategies to Counter Them.

Apply the strategies below and hopefully sooner than later, we get to the place where age discrimination in the workplace fades to the recognition of the value Boomers bring to the table!

STEREOTYPE	STRATEGY
Have Reduced Learning Capacity	• This is a common judgement about older workers and the Canadian Centre for Occupational Health and Safety (2012) advise us that: "Everyone, at every age, thinks and learns differently. These cognitive functions -- how someone learns and thinks -- are very dependent on the individual, and the experiences they have had during their lifetime."[6] • You have worked many years and accumulated skills, experience and knowledge that will provide value for an employer. Continue to demonstrate your ability to adapt and learn new things. Life-long learning is required in the modern labor market. • Think of ways to solve problems in the workplace or increase efficiency.

Possess Outdated Skills	• Upgrade your skills as required including communication, academic, job related coursework, obtaining tickets, designations and others. • Spend time staying current and learning new technology. Doing this will put you in the know and up to date. Employers have started to hire online through social media sites and evidence of a digital presence is expected in certain occupational sectors.
Are Resistant to Change	• Workplace changes are occurring at an accelerated rate, requiring us to adopt and learn how to apply these on the fly. • There is a need to keep an open mind and work collaboratively within the evolving and diverse workforce. Being an older worker does not automatically earn us respect and if this is an attitude we present, it will create conflict. • There is a move towards emotional-social intelligence and the importance of relationship building to create change.
Demand Higher Wages	• Older workers can be seen as a poor investment because they won't remain with a company long enough to get a return on their training costs. Indicate long-term commitment if possible.

Demand Higher Wages	• Let potential employers know that you are flexible and will negotiate and integrate with the pay and benefit scales. • Find contract work, many employers are not offering long term employment.
Demonstrate Slower Decision-Making	• This stereotype varies from individual to individual, whether you are a generation X, Y or Boomer.
Have Lower Productivity	• There is the belief that medical issues impact attendance and productivity, require frequent doctor visits and time off and that older workers are physically slow moving, have low energy and unable to sustain long hours of work. • An older worker may have a health condition. Younger workers can also have health concerns or low energy levels. Focus on a wellness lifestyle to maintain your vitality and wellbeing.

The Demand for Older Workers

The demand for the skills and attributes that older workers possess is increasing.

A stereotype may apply to certain older workers, but this is the exception, according to Kacey Stapleton (2009) who states: "In fact, the opposite of these stereotypes is usual true. Older workers have more experience. They need less training, are less accident prone, have longer attention spans, and are more detail oriented. They've honed better communication skills, and have more pride in their work. Younger workers might be conflicted between work and family—work life balance. Older employees usually are reaching a point in their lives where they may have fewer responsibilities outside work."[7]

The predicted increasing demand for older workers bodes well for unretired Boomers that fit the bill.

The U.S. Administration on Aging reports that: "retirement patterns are changing among America's 78 million baby boomers and this trend is expected to result in an unprecedented number of 50-plus workers participating in the workforce of the 21st century, and an increasing need for the availability of senior jobs."[8]

To ensure a productive workplace for an aging workforce, a factsheet written by the New Zealand, Department of Labor recommends that: "As the age profile of workplaces change, providing a safe, healthy and stimulating work environment for older workers is becoming more important for businesses. Employers should consider three key aspects:

- Flexibility in employment arrangements– like providing scheduling choices to allow for part-time work, catering for caring responsibilities or avoiding night work

- Suitable Ergonomics– such as good lighting, control of noise, and minimizing or eliminating heavy lifting

- Up-skilling Opportunities–make sure that all workers, regardless of age, have access to staff development and training."[9]

Granted, not all employers will be open to hiring and training older workers, or be willing to move beyond their beliefs regarding age and performance. Becoming informed of stereotypes and making changes as required, will enable you to stay current and relevant. It will also increase the odds of staying gainfully employed.

The forecast labor shortage, abolishment of mandatory retirement and other changes pave the way for age discrimination to disappear over time.

The modern evolving workplace is becoming multi-cultural, inter-generational and inclusive of ability, gender and sexual orientation. It is exciting to witness these changes in the labor market.

All generations bring different talents and abilities to the table as so aptly described in this quote:

Young men are fitter to invent than to judge;
fitter for execution than for counsel;
and fitter for new projects than for settled business.
Francis Bacon

You have now read the first two chapters in the occupational series titled: *Work Stressors And Mental Health and Hitting It Head On – Dealing With Ageism.*

Next up is *Career Management for Employees*, which looks at managing the three common employment situations Boomers may find themselves in.

"Keep on trucking," as my 93-year-old mom says, and I excuse her for using a dated expression!

CAREER MANAGEMENT FOR EMPLOYEES

Chapter Fifteen

The best way to predict the future is to create it.
Abraham Lincoln

Career management and career planning next, are key chapters to staying employed and fall within the occupational dimension of a Complete Life Wellness Plan™.

According to the Business Dictionary, career management is the: "Lifelong, self-monitored process of career planning that involves choosing and setting personal goals, and formulating strategies for achieving them."[1]

When we take an active role in our careers, it increases the probability that we will experience greater growth, financial security and/or occupational wellness.

Over my years of working in the employment field, I have met with many individuals, especially Boomers, and assisted them as best I could with their career difficulties. In doing so, I have been privileged to hear and learn from their stories.

I'd like to share a few of these comments:

- "I am frustrated knowing that I work hard five days a week and with the money I'm earning and saving, it will not be enough for a good retirement. What can I do?"

- "Sometimes my life reminds me of an hourglass that is running out of sand, and when it does I will no longer be healthy enough to work or have enough money saved to stop or both."

- "I love working and want to continue as long as I can. My wife says I have to do so to keep out of her hair!"

- "It's been decades since I wrote my last resume and I wouldn't know how to start, let alone go for an interview."

- "After being hammered in the market downturn in 2007/2008 and losing 35% of my net worth and at this stage in my life, I have no choice but to keep working past 65 and into my early 70's."

- "Knowing that I want and need to keep working past 65, I make sure to live a healthy lifestyle and try not to sweat the small stuff."

All of the preceding individuals would benefit from a Complete Life Wellness Plan™. At the risk of repeating myself, when you read these comments it is evident that the occupational dimension is involved but also other dimensions. Can you spot them?

To move further into the contents of this chapter, let's clarify some common terms used in career management and how the world of work has changed.

The word career has numerous definitions and for the purposes of The Un-Retirement Guide™ it refers "to a series of jobs an individual has over his or her lifetime."

> **Career -** Dawn Rosenberg McKay (2014) a career planning expert, explains that a: "Career refers to a series of jobs an individual has over his or her lifetime. These jobs may reflect an upward trajectory, meaning that one will have increasing responsibilities, compensation and more prestige-ious titles with each subsequent position. Alterna-

tively, none of this may be true. Some people's careers are filled with unrelated jobs, or an individual may not experience upward progression, but instead may stay at the same level throughout his or her entire working life."[2]

Job - In its *Planning Your Career Workbook,* the NWT Literacy Council (2012)[3] explains that: "A Job is a paid position requiring a group of specific attributes and skills that enable a person to perform tasks in an organization either part-time or full-time for a short or long duration. An occupation is a group of similar jobs for which people usually have to develop skills and knowledge. An occupation is a specific category of work. A person can have several jobs within an occupation. They can adapt their knowledge and skills to a variety of positions. Examples of occupations include electrician, engineer and teacher."

On the Balanced Life SA (2011) website, an article on integrative life planning informs us that "The world of work known to us today is vastly different from the one our parents and their parents knew. In the course of the previous century, it was common practice to leave school, be trained in a certain discipline, find a job, and retire in the same company forty years later." [4]

Fluid Careers - Susan Imel (2003) writes about the changing nature of careers: "Once thought to be linear in nature with a natural progression up the ladder, careers are now considered to be much more fluid, nonlinear, and unstable. Depending on the individual and the organization, the later career stage *can be a period of growth, maintenance, or decline.*

Even career stages, once thought to be fairly predictable, are being re-examined, revealing that in the middle and later career years, an individual's needs and career concerns change more dynamically than in the past, and continuous learning is required for success. In theory, the late career stage has traditionally meant adjustment into retirement, but in current practice job involvement continues, with little or no physical decline evident."[5]

The Un-Retirement Guide™ supports that the best strategy *to stay gainfully employed* is proactively managing our employment situation, and this is discussed in the remainder of the chapter.

Career Management

The three common employment situations that Boomers may find themselves in that require career management are:

1) You want to stay employed in your current job.
2) Job searching while employed.
3) Job searching while unemployed.

Background on these three employment situations are provided next. See if you identify with any of the descriptions that follow.

1. You want to stay employed in your current job

Staying in your current job is thought by many career camps to be the best option for Boomers to remain employed. This is also dependent on whether it meets your financial needs, not too boring and isn't excessively stressful, in which case job searching while employed may be necessary.

Due diligence needs to be taken with your income while employed to make any efforts to reach financial independence count. Gambling, or fast women or men, is only allowed in moderation!

This can be a time when older workers find themselves with decreased work mobility and locked into their current job. This is especially true if efforts to continue learning and or upgrading have not been pursued and we possess obsolete and/or limited transfer-able skills.

Successfully keeping a job in today's labor market requires more than just showing up every day. To add value to your employer, I believe it is necessary to pursue career growth. The amount of upgrading and/or skill development undertaken will obviously depend on what kind of work you do.

Ongoing efforts to stay relevant and current in your job/occupation are a wise use of your time though, and preferably a match for your interests and aptitudes. This will also position you better for finding other work, if job loss does occur.

The first step towards staying current in today's job market is to determine what categories of your resume require sprucing up. Are there skills that need updating in your current job and/or occupation? Consider building on your strengths, which includes skills you already possess, interests and talents.

Career growth while employed includes:

In-house and /or **training** outside of work hours that could be funded by your employer, yourself or cost-shared. If other life roles present a scheduling conflict, then on-the-job training is preferred.

Outside of work, there are different formats such as online or distance learning and evening courses available.

If the cost of training presents a problem, then it could be managed creatively to keep costs down. Several possibilities are on the job training, volunteering (see below) or having a workplace mentor.

1. Lorraine Rinker (2009) recommends: "**Volunteering** on Advisory Boards – actively participating on an advisory board where you can lend your functional expertise gives you access to a dynamic knowledge and experience base where you are solving real problems in real time. Interaction in this venue will provide you with feedback about your intent and ability to remain relevant in your chosen field of expertise."[6]

2. In addition to a person's knowledge and occupational hard skills, **soft or people skills** are becoming a requirement. Programs that improve our social/emotional intelligence and ability to interact with others such as Toastmasters or conflict resolution training will develop our soft skills.

3. A level of **computer literacy** is needed in most occupations. A "digital footprint" (cool phrase) may also be expected by certain employers. A personal website and presence on relevant social media channels such as career forums or related groups is evidence of this.

It's best not to leave upgrading until the last minute, it takes time and continuous small steps, but never too late!

The next two employment situations involve the job search process.

2. Job Searching While Employed

The following is not an exhaustive list but covers many of the reasons to job search while employed.

- If you have knowledge or suspect that you are being let go, (this could be due to a pending downsizing, being fired or other reason).

- No room for advancement.

- Making a career change.

- Being overworked.

- Stressful and ineffective management style.

- Difficult relationship with the boss.

- Contributions are not being recognized.

- Need better compensation and benefits.

- Not a good fit with an organization.

- The financial instability of an organization.

If searching for a job becomes necessary while employed, certain precautions are necessary. You don't want to lose the job you have before a new one is obtained! This also involves personal integrity and not burning bridges. The following suggestions will help in this phase of your career management.

- Pay for your own paper, postage, fax costs and any job search activities would be carried out on your own time.

- Keep the job search to yourself, not sharing it with work colleagues.

- Make any calls, emails, faxes, social media activity concerning your job search from a non-work computer or location.

- Take time off for interviews, or if possible schedule them for your lunch break or after hours. Make certain your workload is under control as best possible when taking time off for interviews, and networking activities.

- Keep a change of clothes for interviewing during lunch or after work in your car or elsewhere for a quick change. Doing this will not arouse suspicion by your supervisor or colleagues and indicates integrity.

- Before an interview situation, thought should be given to why you're applying and that providing a reference from your current employer isn't appropriate at this time.

3. Job Searching While Unemployed

Last but certainly not least, are those unretired Boomers that have lost their jobs recently, or been job searching for a period of time without success.

The best time to look for work is before you become unemployed, which is just what you want to hear! Often the writing is on the wall, but we can also be blindsided and unaware that our job was in jeopardy.

I've been through what was referred to as a rightsizing, and in denial it was actually going to happen until the final day. I did wonder why the furniture was slowly disappearing though and that there were ongoing small meetings with sad faces! It would have been in my best interests if I'd started the job search process while still employed.

Losing a Job

This is one of those situations in our lives when seeking help is advisable. There are public and private career advisors, counsellors, therapists and coaches available to support you through a job loss and transition to re-employment.

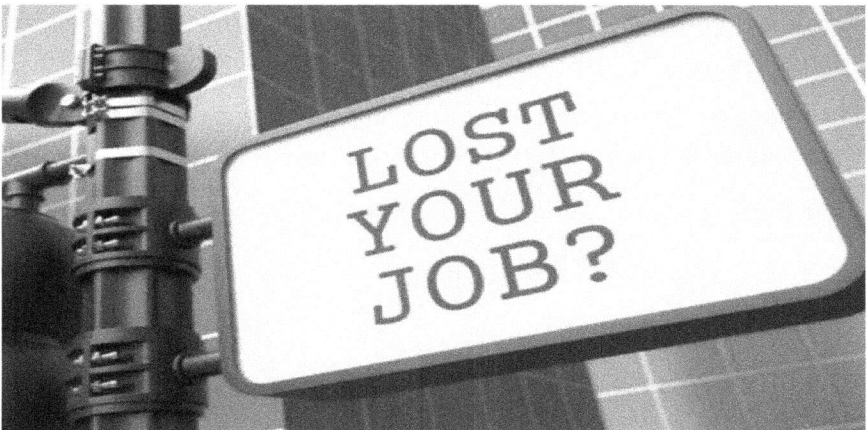

Job loss and searching for new work is challenging for workers of all ages. For an older worker, it can be a foreign landscape, especially if they were employed for many years (decades) in their last job.

Workers have rights regarding unfair employment practices and if this is the case, checking what the employment standards are for the state or province you live in, is a worthwhile action to take.

Some common job loss scenarios are due to:

- Through layoff as in downsizing/rightsizing.

- Forced early retirement (age discrimination?)

- Disabled either on or off the job.

- Failure to keep current and relevant and *let go* (interesting phrase!)

- Terminated for poor job performance (online shopping on EBay), absenteeism (golfing) or presenteeism (staring out the window).

Dismissal from your job is number 8 out of 43 major stressful life events that can contribute to illness according to the Holmes and Rahe stress scale.[7] So be aware of the possibility of an emotional reaction, and take time for self-care.

Grief is a common reaction after job loss. Shock, anger, denial, shame, worry, sadness can be some of the feelings experienced.

There are a number of personal changes related to job dismissal that may be encountered including the following:

- decreased income and possible inability to cover expenses

- our identity related to the type of work performed is lost

- self-esteem and confidence can be diminished

- the routine of how you spent your time during work is disrupted

- financial and emotional security derived from working is suspended

- daily social contact in the workplace is missing

- any purpose and meaning derived from our job is absent

The points above demonstrate it's important to have interests, meaning and connection outside of our jobs. Work can be a powerful influence on our identity and something we need to be aware of. A strong work ethic is something that is valued in our western culture, but who often benefits the most from this?

When we become unemployed, mixed feelings will often result. I felt relieved but vulnerable and wondered how I would ever get another job as good as the one I had. In hindsight, this attachment proved to be more connected to the notion of security than the actual working conditions.

This is the ideal time to prioritize and develop **THE FOUR FOUND-ATIONAL LIFESTYLE HABITS**. Sorry if I sound like a broken record on this point, but during stressful times the benefits will far outweigh any effort.

Preparing for a Job Search

There will be a period of time needed following job loss to **build resilience** and get back into fighting form. To assist in this, under-standing and applying basic stress management techniques will lessen the impact as found in Chapter 7.

Asking for help, such as meeting with a mental health counsellor to assist with any adjustment problems may be required. Like career counsellors or coaches, therapists are publically or privately avail-able. I have used both after losing a job to navigate a course correction and found it invaluable, and later landed a great new job!

The time following job loss is challenging and requires that you *accept* what happened and move forward in managing your career.

Many have said and it will sound cliché, but looking back it was one of the best things that ever happened to me.

If you were not happy at a job it makes it easier, but either way, life goes on and the wolves must be kept away from the door!

As soon as your job ends or preferably before, you need to manage the transition to unemployment. This may be a time when you least feel like doing this, but it will restore a sense of control and position you for the job search.

Hunker Down

What follows are suggestions to increase your sense of control and ready you to start your job search:

1. Check the details of any severance package received for tax implications and how it will be paid out. Will benefits like medical, dental or life insurance continue for a period of time after termination? Arrange for personal-family medical coverage as needed.

2. Ask for a letter(s) of reference or preferably recommendation that acknowledge your accomplishments and skills from your manager or supervisor. This is something you can write and have the employer sign, which they are agreeable to in many cases.

3. Obtain a record of employment or separation slip and apply for un/employment insurance benefits immediately, if eligible.

4. Take a snapshot of your (family) finances to understand your cash flow. *You may not like your financial picture, but you will know exactly what it is or isn't.* Create a monthly budget and more importantly track spending. This can be done with a pen and paper or by using computer software designed to manage personal finances. It's an area where it is wise to work with a financial planner and/or debt counsellor.

5. Discuss with family and friends your change in employment status to clarify your situation and foster a supportive network, and get over any embarrassment.

Job searching, is a challenging activity many of us go through more than once, over the course of our work history and is covered in detail in the next chapter.

The days of one job and a gold watch at the end are mostly gone, and in my opinion that's a good thing!

It can be a bit of a jungle out there and all the more reason to carry out career planning, the next topic.

Starting the career planning process

As a matter of review, the three common employment situations Boomers find themselves in that require career management are:

1) You want to stay employed in your current job.

2) Job searching while employed.

3) Job searching while unemployed.

Goal Setting

To begin the career planning process, we need to set two goals only, as employment situations 2 and 3 both involve job searching and these goals are:

1. Pursue growth in your current job, or

2. Conduct a targeted job search

In the next chapter we take these two career goals and run them through a **Three Step Career Planning** process. Simply put, this will enable us to come up with strategies for achieving these goals.

Raring to go?

CAREER PLANNING AND CONDUCTING A TARGETED JOB SEARCH

Chapter Sixteen

Don't forget to belly breathe. Have fun.
Remember that working does not go on forever.
There are those who believe in reincarnation though,
and if that's true, that would allow for further
career planning!
Brian Lukyn

In my early job searching days I used to send out piles of resumes for job postings I had varying degrees of qualification for, sometimes very little. I also sent resumes to companies where there were no job openings advertised, and I became skilled at writing cover letters to explain why they should hire me. I once received a letter from an employer I had sent a resume and cover letter that stated "that they had no openings for a person with my qualifications and doubted they ever would!" This bolstered my self-confidence during lean times.

I experienced bouts of unemployment where I needed a job, any job and took temporary ones to survive. A few examples include: laborer on a railway line maintenance crew (hammering spikes); firewood splitter; and deckhand on a salmon packer.

These were short term work experiences that provided valuable lessons, which included making me determined to find a better way to manage my career and conduct a job search. This chapter is the result of the promises I made to myself in those days when I didn't know what I needed to know, and now share with my readers.

Three Step Career Planning

As determined at the end of Chapter 15, the two career goals are:

- pursue growth in your current job,

- conduct a targeted job search

Planning for the achievement of a career goal is a straightforward process. The three steps used for career planning are briefly described in the next section and more fully later in this chapter.

Steps

1. Self-Assessment

In this step we learn about our skills, values, interests, personality traits and other relevant background information. This provides the basis for making informed decisions in the planning process. The results of the self-assessment are summarized in a document called a Personal

Career Profile which is also used to determine what labor market information we look for in step 2.

2. Labor Market Research

The information you are seeking will depend on what your career goal is. For our purposes it would concentrate on either; educational areas for growth and occupations/employers that fit our targeted job search criteria.

When the labor market research is completed, the information is narrowed down and a decision is made which training/courses or occupations/jobs are best to include in your action plan in step 3.

3. The Action Plan

An action plan sets out the path you take to achieve your career goal. It can involve exploring further options, asking others for feedback or other and identifying what order to do things in. In our situations the intent of the action plan is that you *stay or become gainfully employed*.

The Business Dictionary provides a concise definition of career planning, which is described as a: "structured exercise undertaken to identify one's objectives, marketable skills, strengths, and weaknesses, etc., as a part of one's career management."[1]

This structured exercise makes up the contents of the remainder of the chapter.

I have included a flowchart for Three Step Career Planning for you to refer to, a picture is worth a thousand words and all that jazz.

THREE STEP CAREER PLANNING PROCESS

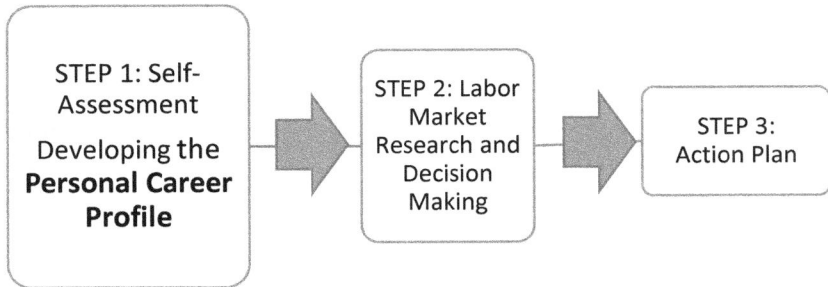

| STEP 1: Self-Assessment

Developing the **Personal Career Profile** | → | STEP 2: Labor Market Research and Decision Making | → | STEP 3: Action Plan |

Enough said as an introduction to **Three Step Career Planning**, let's begin!

Step One: **Self-Assessment and the Personal Career Profile**

It is advantageous to assess who we are as a worker, especially if you're a Boomer who after many years of working in the same job, is suddenly unemployed. This step also includes identifying any barriers that might restrict a successful return to work.

The Work-BC website advises that: "By clarifying what you want from a career, self-assessment can help you avoid false starts and disappointments in life. It can increase your confidence that you are on the right path and lead to personal and professional success and satisfaction. That's why self-assessment is your powerful first step to making career decisions."[2]

A self-assessment can be started on your own using online or hard copy resources, but in my experience it is best if you get the assistance of a career counsellor. They have various tools and resources for creating your personal career profile.

Typically, there are five categories used in a self-assessment. Three more have been added for the purposes of The Un-Retirement Guide™ that include work experience; education and training; and barriers to employment. This will allow for a more comprehensive self-assessment and basis for career planning.

1. Transferable Skills and Personal Qualities

There is confusion around what skills are, due to the various names they are given. A concise definition from the Merriam Webster dictionary defines skill as: "the ability to do something that comes from training, experience, or practice."[3]

It is important to remember that skills can be developed on or off the job.

For the sake of simplicity, job skills are best described as hard or soft. An excerpt from a post written by Lei Han, a career success expert, defines the different types of job skills required by individuals in the labor market. I have shortened her excellent post and if you are interested in reading the full version please visit the Chapter 17 notes in the appendices for this information.

Ms. Han breaks hard and soft job skills down into the following:

"**Hard skills** – These are trade skills and subject matter expertise, like programming, accounting, financial analysis, or chemical engineering that we need to perform our job.

Soft Skills – People skills – These are the skills we use to interact with others at work. Examples of people skills include communications and interpersonal skills as well as skills to manage upwards and deal with office politics.

Soft Skills – Self management skills – These are the skills to help us manage self-perception and our reactions to adverse situations."[4]

On the subject of hard and soft skills Alison Doyle informs us that: "While certain hard skills are necessary for any position, employers are looking increasingly for job applicants with particular soft skills. This is because, while it is easy for an employer to train a new employee in a particular hard skill (such as how to use a certain computer program), it is much more difficult to train an employee in a soft skill (such as patience). ``[5]

Personal Qualities

Often overlooked and in addition to hard and soft skills, Randall S. Hansen et al adds: "Of equal importance to skills are the values, personality traits, and personal characteristics that employers seek.

A few examples of personal qualities are *work ethic, professionalism, honesty and a positive attitude*. Personal qualities are also transferable.

Look for ways to weave examples of these characteristics into your resume, cover letters, and answers to interview questions."[6]

Keep in mind that greater importance is being placed on soft skills and personal qualities in today's labor market.

What are transferable skills?

Transferable or portable skills are those hard and soft skills that as the name implies can be moved between jobs and/or occupations. Identifying the skills you own and where a skill gap may exist is an important part of a self-assessment.

The Laurier Career Development Center emphasizes that: "The ability to understand and describe your skills with depth and insight is key to effective job search preparation."[7]

Describing your skills with depth and insight also applies to those individuals, whose goal is *keeping your current job*.

Identifying Transferable Skills

Soft and hard skills have been developed and accumulated by Boomers to varying degrees, over the length of their career path and other experiences. This also applies to personal qualities that employers value in today's job market. We may not be aware of our own skills and qualities and need assistance finding out what they are.

There are career instruments/assessments and exercises available that help identify skills we have and match them to occupations or job descriptions. Don Georgevich, on the Job Interview Tools website, advises a: "career aptitude test will hone in on an individual's strengths and key skills similar to job aptitude test. In this manner, it helps to pinpoint the jobs that they would be good at. For example, a typical career aptitude test would ask questions about verbal and numerical reasoning, language skills, perception, technical skills and special abilities."[8]

There are also simple methods to get started identifying skills such as the SkillScan Card Sort where: "This inventory features a hands-on card sort to help pinpoint your strengths and skill preferences. It provides you with words to help define your skills for resumes and cover letters, and for your own career decision-making."[9]

The Importance of Transferable Skills

Often individuals find they have more skills than they were aware of after completing a thorough self-assessment. **Knowing what transferable skills you own and can market is empowering.**

When writing transferable skill statements for your resume, they need to be connected to measurable achievements to obtain maximum results, when marketing your skills to a prospective employer.

145

A post on the Job-Interview-Site.com discusses the significance of transferable skills stating that: "When a person is changing jobs or careers it is easy to become worried and unsure about how they will compete with others who have already have direct experience in the job(s) you are applying for. When a person takes the approach of using a transferable skills checklist to promote themselves on their resume, they increase the likelihood of being chosen to for the position because their resume reflects a great deal of necessary skills. In these instances, many times the missing experience in that field is dwarfed by the mounting skills you have. So once you have made a decision to change careers or jobs, the first place you should start building your resume is from the skills you have not the skills you need."[10]

To continue with this topic, I share the following on the versatility of transferable skills.

Joe Turner, author of *Job Search Secrets Unlocked* and *Paycheck 911* advises that we are not our job title and to: "Begin by viewing your work experience as a set of competencies and roles that you have mastered and that can be useful from one occupation or industry to another. This is what is meant by the term transferable skills. They afford you versatility and adaptability and they open up new possibilities."[11]

Job searchers then can use their transferable skills to apply for jobs they have no direct experience in. This may be hard to wrap one's head around, and at the same time offers exciting possibilities!

2. Work Values

Work values refer to those fundamental beliefs and ideas you have about your occupation or job. They are an important part of who you are and if they are not factored in when choosing a career or job/occupation, your chances of finding work satisfaction are lowered.

Values are often described as intrinsic or extrinsic, the first to do with the nature of the work, such as any purpose derived or contribution to others and the second concerns the physical work environment, potential earnings or other.

There is a self-assessment tool called a work value inventory which a career counsellor can administer that is straightforward to take and involves ranking a list of values by order of significance for you and then picking the top 5 or 6.

Lastly, our work values may differ from our non-work values or what an employer values in an employee!

The top 6 work values for me are:

- **Helping others**: providing assistance to individuals or groups
- **Autonomy:** working freely with little or no supervision
- **Creativity:** using my own ideas
- **Variety:** doing different activities
- **Compensation:** meets my financial needs
- **Leisure:** having adequate time away from work to attend to non-work needs

3. Interests

Interests are another important category of a self-assessment and are succinctly described in a post on the SaskNetWork web-site: "Interests, your likes, and dislikes, are an important part of career choice, and are related to values and often to skills and abilities. Most people who enjoy their work have some personal interest in what they are doing."[12]

As with work values there are self-assessment tools available to help discover an individual's interests such as the Strong Interest Inventory (SII) which is the most popular one used today. The Strong Interest Inventory requires the individual to answer 291 items regarding their preferences or interests in relation to occupations, subject areas, activities, leisure activities, people and characteristics. From this inventory your interests are summarized, ranked and matched to occupations that can be researched in Step 2.

4. Personality

This is best explored through a personality assessment; free versions can be found online and in career agencies. The Myers-Briggs Type Indicator is the primary assessment of personality type and it: "describes people's preferences for interacting with others, gathering information, making decisions and organizing their lives."[13]

5. Aptitude

Aptitude is a term that is confusing to many, but included in a personal career profile. Its importance to career planning is described by experts at the Johnson O'Connor Research Foundation as: "Your aptitudes have little to do with knowledge or culture, or education, or interests. They have to do with heredity. Aptitude testing is an invaluable tool for making career and educational decisions."[14]

Here is another insight on aptitudes as posted by Dawn Rosenberg McKay, Career Planning Expert: "Aptitude tests can help you figure out what your natural talents are. One may have an aptitude for math or writing or may have manual dexterity or good spatial abilities, for example. You can have multiple aptitudes. It is important to keep in mind that even if you have an aptitude for something, that doesn't mean you will necessarily like it."[15]

Aptitude tests are available online but best taken through a career agency or private provider.

6. Work Experience

What paid work have you done in the past? Go back to your first job, work experience beyond 10 years won't be directly listed on a resume, but used for the purpose of skill identification and increasing awareness regarding your work history.

Include start to end date, name of employer and position held with a brief description, to the best of your ability.

Volunteer experience can also be added in this category under a sub-heading.

7. Education and Training

List all education completed back to your high school years, as much as you can remember.

Include start to end date, name of school, program/course and certificates or other recognition of your efforts. You don't need to put down dates for education beyond 10 years

If you are currently attending an educational program that is not completed, add this now.

8. Barriers to Employment

Elisabeth H. Sanders-Park explains that a: "A barrier to employment is anything that may be used to screen a candidate out. Barriers include no work history, too much work history, and even a successful career with a single company for many years. They include, too little, too much or lack of specific education. It's the way we look, where we live, how we talk, having too many children or not enough teeth, over-qualification and arrogance, immigrant status and shyness, and so much more. Anything that could result in the candidate not getting the job is a barrier."[16]

Iseekjobs, an online career, education and job resource advises that: "All job seekers need to focus on their qualifications and positive traits, not on their barriers. If an employer asks about your barrier in a job interview, be prepared to talk about how it will not affect your ability to be a good employee."[17]

Identify any barriers confronting you that may hinder reaching your goal(s). With the assistance of a career counsellor you could develop a strategy to manage these parts of your life. Certain barriers can be sorted out using common sense or with the help of family and friends or may involve the assistance of a therapist, debt counsellor or other resource person.

A description of potential barriers, along with the results from the other 7 categories of the self-assessment are transferred to the Personal Career Profile Table below.

The Personal Career Profile becomes a document that simplifies and organizes the planning process. It is a baseline that greatly increases knowing who you are as a worker/person according to the eight categories, what you have to offer and where you may need upgrading to stay or become gainfully employed. This makes creating a resume and cover letters easier and more authentic, with the end result something you own, not just a bunch of canned words and phrases.

Having a document that lists your personal career profile is empowering and could be useful in other situations such as job interviews.

Personal Career Profile Table

PART A:

List your 5 Greatest Job Skills and Personal Qualities:

1.	1.
2.	2.
3.	3.
4.	4.
5.	5.

PART B:

List your Top 5 Work Values:

1.
2.
3.
4.

PART C:

List your Top 5 Interests

1.
2.
3.
4.
5.

PART D:

Go on-line or to a career centre and complete a personality questionnaire. Then summarize your personality type, and major comments below:

My Personality Type is:

Describe in more detail:

_____
_____
_____
_____
_____
_____
_____

PART E:

Describe your Top 5 Aptitudes (or less) below:

1.
2.
3.
4.
5.

PART F:

Summarize your Work Experience as follows.

Start to end dates	Name of employer	Position held with a brief description

_____
_____
_____
_____
_____
_____
_____

PART G:

Summarize your Education and Training back to and including high school education below.

Start to end dates	Name of school/provider	Program/course and certificates etc.

_____
_____
_____
_____
_____
_____
_____
_____
_____
_____

PART H:

List any Barriers to Employment that you may have:

_____
_____
_____
_____
_____
_____
_____
_____

By now you will have completed your Personal Career Profile. The results from the exercises above are best written down on paper or typed into a computer document, as space to do so in the Guidebook is limited. This is also a good time to put together a portfolio, to store the information collected to date and keep everything in one place.

153

Step Two: **Labor Market Research**

With your Personal Career Profile in hand, let's look at how we move forward to step 2 for each of the career goals.

a) Pursuing growth in your current job

After completing the Personal Career Profile in Step 1 you may, among other possible options, decide that training is necessary to address a skill gap. It will require labor market research in Step 2 to locate the course or program that fits your needs. This research is narrowed down and decisions are made as to which learning opportunities are best for use in your action plan in Step 3.

b) Conduct a targeted job search

The focus of the labor market research in Step 2 is the industries, sectors, occupations and employers that match your personal career profile and job search criteria. This research is also narrowed down and decisions are made as to which employers and occupations/jobs will be used in your action plan in step 3.

Because of the challenges Boomers face who are searching for work, the information in the remainder of this chapter concentrates on how to conduct a targeted job search.

I may address this later on my website but for now, those individuals whose career goal is pursuing growth in your current job, please ☺ complete the remainder of the career planning process with a career professional, if necessary. There is also a fairly thorough discussion on pursuing career growth in Chapter 15.

I highly recommend you read this chapter though, to help understand the labor market and job searching. There is always the possibility that your current job takes a turn for the worst, and you will need *to conduct a targeted job search*, while employed.

Labor market research is a skill every modern job searcher and career planner needs to develop.

The labor market is defined in the Collins dictionary as:" When you talk about the labor market, you are referring to all the people who are able to work and want jobs in a country or area, in relation to the number of jobs there are available in that country or area."[18]

What is Labor Market Information?

Settlement.org provides newcomers with information and resources to settle in Ontario, Canada. This includes labor market information, which they advise consists of finding answers to questions such as these.

1. "What skills employers are looking for?

2. Which industries are hiring?

3. Where to find employers who are hiring?

4. What working conditions are like for specific industries?

5. What education and training you need for specific jobs?

6. What factors can stop you from getting a job?

7. Which job areas are growing in the future?"[19]

Step 2 requires keeping the questions above in mind and others, while researching the industries, occupations, employers and job titles that match the criteria of your personal career profile. This would be accomplished through hard copy and online sources, networking and information interviews.

The reasoning behind researching the labor market is explained in the following excerpt from a past issue of the Occupational Outlook: "It is important to use labor market information in career planning because decisions about paid employment often involve a compromise between what you would most enjoy doing and what the labor market needs and wants. Remember there is no such thing as a correct career decision. The goal is to make an informed choice. When you have access to facts and new ideas you are better able to make an informed choice."[20]

Where do you begin?

Start with the industries you are interested and/or experienced in and narrow them down as you begin researching labor market information (or LMI). Are there trends affecting these industries that will result in growth or decline in the years ahead? Are there similar occupations within these industries that are reasonable matches for your personal career profile? LMI for various industries can be found on government or other online sites. There are also industry specific association and organization websites and annual conferences or other gatherings that would be beneficial to attend to network and gather LMI.

Our transferable skills allow us flexibility in today's job market, where a candidate may be hired with no direct experience. We need to get away from defining ourselves by a job title only. This allows a different and better way of looking at the process of job searching.

LMI from the Government of Canada advises that: "To make sense of current trends in the labor market, it is important to focus on occupations rather than jobs, and on skills rather than the specific tasks of individual jobs. Identifying the fundamental similarities of skills within an occupation allows users to examine concepts such as occupational mobility, transferability of skills and career shifts in today's labor market."[21]

Mary Marino, founder of EmploymentPipeline.com, a US job search resource you should check out, states that: "Conversely, searching by occupational categories is a much better way to perform your job search. Sure, searching by job titles can narrow your search. However, it could narrow it too much."[22]

Ms. Marino also recommends using a widget her company offers called an "Occupation Pipeline" which allows job seekers to "perform broader searches by sourcing occupations and employers, rather than job titles."[23]

An excellent LMI site in Canada is the National Occupational Classification (NOC) which: "organizes over 40,000 job titles into 500 occupational group descriptions."[24]

Attached to the NOC is the *Career Handbook*, which is the counselling component and provides: "information on aptitudes, interests, involvement with data/people/things, physical activities, environmental conditions, education/training indicators, career progression and work settings."[25]

The U.S. Bureau of Labor Statistics is also a great source of LMI to start your research. It contains 840 detailed occupations where: "Workers are classified into occupational categories based upon work performed, skills, education, training, and credentials. Two examples of occupations are accountants and auditors; and janitors and cleaners. Some occupations are found in just one or two industries; however, many occupations are found in a large number of industries."[26]

Similar to the Canadian career handbook is the Occupational Outlook Handbook in the US which covers: "the nature of the work, education and training requirements, advancement opportunities, employment, salary, and ten-year job outlook for hundreds of occupations."[27]

Continue narrowing down your labor market research from the industry to the occupational/job level and develop a list of target employers that appear to be a good fit. Identify the relevant departments and individuals who have the capacity to hire, which in bigger companies may be the human resource manager. Getting their contact information and title is important for future use. Company websites, yellow pages, social media sites such as LinkedIn and association websites are some of the resources available to find this critical information. Last but not least, is phoning the company directly to ask for the name of the individual who can hire and their phone number and email, if it feels right to ask.

Keep precise notes on employer contact information, their business model and any other relevant aspects. Demonstrating knowledge of what a company does, who the players are, and what the problems or pain areas are would establish credibility in an informational or job interview.

Once you have gained the industry, occupational and employer data, it is time to move to the networking phase. This involves speaking directly with those people working in your field of interest through informational interviews.

Informational Interviews

The most valuable intel comes from meeting and talking to people who are performing the job you're interested in, or have the power to hire for these positions. You might be saying to yourself as you read these words, I know where this is going! I had a conversation with a teacher once where I asked if he got nervous before teaching a large class of students and he told me; "I still get butterflies but I taught them to fly in formation!" This has stuck in my mind for over 20 years and speaks to being thoroughly prepared and of course remembering to breathe slowly and fully during any meetings, such as an informational interview! With practice they get easier, and may become something you look forward to.

Informational interviewing enables you to meet face-to-face with people who can provide inside intelligence, and/or be a source of referrals and job leads. Following this kind of interview, you may be offered a job at a later date if you leave a favourable impression.

"Informational interviews differ from a job interview due to the nature of the meeting. Job seekers typically initiate the interview in an effort to gain more knowledge about their desired career or an employer they are interested in working for."[28]

An article by The Media School, Journalism Indiana University comments on the reasoning behind informational interviews:

- "To get valuable information. It's a good way to check what you've read, heard and think.

- To learn about a particular organization and industry, how you might fit in and about the problems or needs of the employer. This information will help you direct your qualifications toward the needs of the organization and industry.

- To gain interview experience and confidence by discussing yourself and your career interests with professionals.

- To enlarge your circle of contacts in the field. It is often whom you know or meet that helps get you an internship or job. It's never too early to establish contacts.

- To ask for other referrals (for example: Can you suggest some other people that I might talk to about careers in this field?)"[29]

Now that you have a list of employer's targets and the names of those who can hire, it is time to contact them. This is best accomplished by phone but written correspondence or email can also be used.

It makes it easier if you've been referred by someone, but it may require calling someone you don't know to set up the interview. The challenge of these calls is minimized if you understand what you have to offer in this field and thoroughly research the employer. This is discussed further in Step 3 under Employment Prospecting.

Writing a short personal script or elevator speech for introducing yourself will make the initial contact easier. This can also be used later during a formal job search.

Assistance in preparing for an informational or job interview is a service offered by public career agencies. It is invaluable to participate in an audio or video recorded session beforehand.

I recommend that you take notes during (with permission) and shortly after the interview is over. Jot down business points including any notable remarks made by who you are meeting with. This can be used later during your formal job search with this potential employer or another in the same industry. Try not to leave without a referral and obtain permission to use their name when contacting the referred individual.

Informational interviews are an excellent way to meet potential employers outside of a job interview.

Communicating at the beginning of the call that you want to meet for information purposes only will dissolve any pretext.

Leaving your networking contact card falls within the bounds of "just seeking information" after the interview ends.

Continue to store this information in your career portfolio and keep accurate, legible records.

Sending a brief thank you note shortly afterwards to the individual or industry contact you met with is advisable.

These interviews should be treated as potential gold. This means bringing your "A game" in your grooming and knowing why you are there. The individual you are interviewing with could turn out to be your next boss!

When sufficient labor market research (including informational interviews) has been performed, you should know what industries, sector, occupations and employers you want to target. Ideally these prospects are a close match to your personal career profile and job search criteria. Work that matches our interests is a predictor of satisfaction and success.

Wrapping up Labor Market Research in Step 2

I should add that a targeted job search may be delayed if you determine during the self-assessment in Step 1, that retraining is needed beforehand to address a skill gap.

There are ways around this though:

1. Certain employers (as in my case) may hire on the basis that any upgrading required is completed within a reasonable timeframe after commencing employment.

2. Another strategy is that an employer could hire an applicant with strong soft skills and be willing to overlook a hard skill gap, with the intent of investing in training the individual at a future point. This is a good example of the importance and transferability of soft skills!

Lastly, any barriers identified during the self-assessment that might interfere with a successful targeted job search may need resolving before an individual is "job ready."

The labor market research that you performed is narrowed down and decisions are made as to which employers and occupations/jobs will be pursued in your action plan in step 3.

Step Three: **Action Plan**

A bit of background first on why should we bother to go through the effort of conducting a targeted job search, before we get into the action plan. You don't have to look for a job in this manner, but the rationale behind doing so is explained in the next section.

Hidden Job Market

The active targeted job search is active versus passive in that it requires contacting and marketing yourself to those employers where no job is advertised. The key point to remember is that the employers you target may never advertise publically but still have jobs that need filling. These "hidden jobs" may be in various stages from waiting on funding at year-end to needing to fill a position by the end of the month or now.

The passive method is where no employer contact has been made and resume packages are sent to advertised job postings. It is often the case with this method where you do not hear back that your application was even received. Job searchers do get hired using the passive approach, but the odds of this happening are not high. Applying to advertised job postings without any inside contact, should be included in a job search if it fits your targeted job search criteria and if necessary, to apply for a survival job. But don't sit back and assume that is all you need to do to get a fulfilling and suitable job.

By the time a job opening is advertised, the number of applicants will be large, maybe huge depending on the labor market. This is one of the reasons employers prefer to fill openings through referrals to avoid a flood of applicants. Hiring before jobs are advertised or even fully developed through an inside network is known as the Hidden Job Market.

Many employers prefer to find future employees through referrals from people they trust. Referred individuals have a greater chance of getting an interview and being hired than other applicants. This network is referred to as the hidden job market and according to Job Star, an online resource for job hunters: "80% of all positions are filled without employer advertising. These positions are filled by–or created for–candidates who come to an employer's attention through employee recommendations, referrals from trusted associates, recruiters, or direct contact with the candidate."[30]

If you're on board, now it is time to get out there and make it happen!

Action plan contents and process

I'll change "action plan" to targeted job search action plan from this point on. It would consist of the short-listed employer targets, the job search materials and a schedule of actions to contact employers, follow-up and other activities to secure gainful employment.

The targeted job search process is not a straight line. In the morning we may research labor market information on one employer target and in the afternoon attend a networking meeting for a different one. It requires elbow grease, and being organized. The process repeats itself until a job is landed.

Firming up the short-list of employer targets

By the beginning of Step 3 a list of employers to target has been assembled from the career decisions and labor market research performed in Steps 1 and 2. These prospects have been vetted for growth, location and other criteria established up front, and include the names of the hiring reps and their contact information.

Conduct further research if necessary on these employers, such as obtaining a job description that defines what qualifications are expected to work for their company. Dig deeply and get to know what they do and how they do it. Pay particular attention to their challenges and how your transferable skills might offer a solution for their needs going forward.

The employer targets will need replenishing as some will be dropped for various reasons, such as the employer is waiting on new legislation or funding before any hiring occurs, or you didn't gel with the employer hiring rep. during an information interview and so on.

Before contacting any prospects, it is necessary to prepare customized job search marketing materials. These are the resume and cover letter which are customized for each target and other supporting documents which are discussed next.

Preparing job search marketing materials

A resume is the most important document in your career portfolio. Time and focused effort are required to produce an excellent resume to increase the odds of getting a foot in the door for an information or job interview.

There are 3 styles of resumes in use today: functional, chrono-logical, and the *combination* which is thought to be the best format for older workers when there is a long work history and well-developed skills. This is not to say that the other formats shouldn't be considered, each one has its strengths and weaknesses. The *functional* resume format may be the best choice if: "you're trying to change careers or industries and your past job titles don't relate."[31]

An excellent functional or skills-based resume would hinge on solid transferable skill statements, which also applies to the other formats.

It is one thing to put a list of your skills and strengths down in a cover letter and resume and as mentioned previously, another to acquire: "the ability to understand and describe your skills with depth and insight. ``[32]

You will need to be able to communicate and successfully market these skills in a job interview!

Spending adequate time identifying and learning what your transferable skills are and how they meet the needs of the target employer is vital to job search preparation. Creating transferable skills statements that includes a benefit phrase on how you will assist the employer if they hire you takes time and effort to get right. Once the transferable skill statements are polished, they can be tweaked for different employer targets.

Make the effort to age-proof your resume by going back 10 years only in your work history, use the current phrases for headings, replace a job objective with a summary of qualifications, and highlight recent training and job achievements. It is not required to put down dates for an academic degree, trade certification or other that were obtained decades ago. Getting professional help from a career counsellor who has expertise preparing resumes and cover letters for older workers is recommended and these individuals can usually be found through free, government career agencies.

Online resources like:
http://www.monster.com/ and http://www.quintcareers.com/ that are mentioned below, have been around a long time and are great sites to check out for career management information and tips that include resumes and cover letters.

Concerning cover letters, John Rossheim, Monster senior contributing writer has this to say: "The cover letter is an age-neutral communication that can build a bridge from your impressive career accomplishments to the prospective employer's specific needs and help punch your ticket to a job interview."[33]

Age neutral implies it's an important tool for Boomers. It should also convince the employer to read your resume, highlights your skills and accomplishments, and demonstrates how you meet the needs of a particular company.

Check in with your references to see that they are still available and that you have their correct phone numbers. Discussing what employer(s) you are targeting, and how they might respond to any questions from an employer who calls is wise to do. References can be kept on a separate page and adding "References available upon request" on the resume is not necessary, as it is implied.

I am bringing up the topic of a job search career portfolio again at this point because it may give that extra push that gets a job candidate hired and therefore deserves consideration.

In a post from the Quintessential Careers site, Randall Hansen writes: "What is a job skill, job-search, or career portfolio? It is a job-hunting tool that you develop that gives employers a complete picture of who you are – your experience, your education, your accomplishments, your skill sets – and what you have the potential to become – much more than just a cover letter and resume can provide. You can use your career portfolio in job interviews to showcase a point, to illustrate the depth of your skills and experience, or to use as a tool to get a second interview."[34]

I recommend visiting the nearest career agency to network and take advantage of their employment services. Among other services they offer are: assistance in resume and cover letter preparation; job interviewing practice; networking for job leads; and often free use of phones, faxes, copying, and computers to use in job searching.

Once your resume, cover letter and any other documents are ready it is time to contact your prospects!

Launching an active, targeted job search

By this point you are ready to launch your active targeted job search.

> **Remind yourself each day of your search that even though there is no job advertised by an employer it doesn't mean that no job exists!**

The goal is to get some face time with employer reps that can hire and provide referrals, job leads or employment. This is easier if you have personally met the employer rep. through networking, or been referred by another. If it someone you have no connection to, it will require starting from scratch.

Employment Prospecting

Fortunately, there is a method to access those employer reps you are targeting known as employment or job prospecting. It applies the how, when and what you communicate to market yourself:

1. The how consists of using multiple channels to touch an employer rep. such as the phone, email, social media, written correspondence and fax if appropriate.

2. The when is every 10 days which is thought by some to be a good interval to follow-up between touches without appearing pushy.

3. The what, or content in these communications should be well thought out and compelling, and market how you meet an employer's needs, and applies to all the channels including voicemail. It is strategic to touch base with a series of actions, follow an introduction letter with a phone call and/or email to make certain you reach the hiring rep.

Sending out well-written introduction letters and later custom resumes and cover letters with follow up phone calls and emails to those individuals targeted will get you started. It is not a science, and will require calibrating over the targeted job search campaign.

When your prospecting efforts have succeeded in getting a meeting, the agenda is similar to an informational interview. You are not there to directly ask for employment but to obtain inside industry information, present what you have to offer and gather feedback on how your background could fit in. At the end of the meeting, and if it went well, ask for a referral from the rep. and permission to use his/her name. Follow up thank you letters are sent promptly and this individual then becomes part of your cherished network which you stay *in touch* with tactfully.

Keep your eyes on the goal and try not to be thrown off track if the interviews are not coming as fast as you would like, or you run into a few less than helpful people.

As you actively prospect employers and their hiring reps your network will expand, as will your industry knowledge and access to the hidden job market.

Networking

The word networking as it is applied to a job search can strike fear in the hearts of many. It is still associated with approaching a loud room full of people that are far more successful than we are, or being fed to the lions! The first reaction is to leave as quickly as possible! To lay this to rest, networking is often performed on a one on one basis.

Many people feel a degree of awkwardness around others, especially someone they have never met and I include myself here. These days though, I often feel excited after meeting with new people that I need to speak with to move my life ahead. Like many things, networking requires practice and understanding that people want to help! Read onward for more on surviving the world of networking.

The object of networking is to obtain information on LMI, job leads, new referrals and sometimes being hired on the spot! Unretired Boomers (and others) may be resistant to networking and as a result don't take advantage of, or are unaware of the often large networks they have developed over the years. There are many misconceptions about networking such as "it requires selling oneself," "you need to know the person well," or "nobody has time for my problems" and so on. We all need help at different times and being unemployed can happen to any of us!

A different way of looking at networking is provided by Phyllis Mufson, career expert and business consultant, who advises that: "One of the most difficult aspects of being out of work can be isolation, and for that, networking is an excellent antidote. As you focus on connecting with your network you'll feel less alone. When you reach out to share what you know and help other people with information and support you'll feel a stronger sense of purpose. It won't be long before you'll have a whole circle of people you are contributing to, and being supported by. The effectiveness of your job search will multiply. With hundreds of eyes and ears looking and listening for jobs for you, you'll learn of opportunities you would never have found on your own."[35]

Networking, which includes informational interviews, is a rich source of job leads in the hidden job market. It is regarded as the top method for conducting a professional job search.

If your network's limited, start to practice with family, friends, co-workers and community contacts. This will soon grow to the point where you will get calls from people you don't know! As you network with familiar faces, it will prepare you to approach new people.

Networking with people in the same field of interest makes this process easier and it is best accomplished when the networkers are comfortable and relaxed such as over a lunch or coffee, in a favourite spot.

Part of the intention with networking is obtaining feedback, referrals and labor market information that combined will generate job leads and eventual employment.

During networking conversations, do not ask people directly for work. Express interest in the individual and their career path; offer something in return that is of similar value or effort. When appropriate, a job may be offered or you can ask directly.

This is called networking etiquette and further aspects of it include sending thank you cards following a meeting. Thank you correspondence should be brief and demonstrate your professionalism and gratitude for their time and effort.

Networking will continue until you are employed and relationships with those contacts you choose to keep, maintained afterwards.

Job Search Scheduling

Take a moment and reflect on how you're doing with THE 4 FOUNDATIONAL LIFESTYLE HABITS, including any evidence of a stress response and adjust accordingly. This really is a priority and necessary to increase the odds of a successful job search.

Each week of your active targeted job search campaign should be planned set goals to accomplish with and stay on track.

Unexpectedly, you may have to prepare for an interview on Monday over the weekend, so being flexible and redesigning your job search plan and "work week" may be necessary. Try to work in an organized and efficient manner and enlist a career counsellor or coach for support and expertise.

Keeping accurate records of your progress is essential. Schedule time to: research and identify new employer targets; manage those employer reps you have begun self-marketing to and add new prospects as required; customize resumes and cover letters, write follow up and thank you letters; and attend networking meetings.

These activities will keep you busy and require time management skills and perseverance. Certain days of the week like Monday are not the best day to reach people by phone, so this day could be set aside for other tasks.

Continue with this multipronged approach: steadily researching, networking, prospecting and each will feed into the other, and yield results! Interviews!

Successful Interviewing

In addition to all the effort you have put into your active targeted job search campaign so far, successful interviewing is necessary to land a job and is where you get to show off your soft skills!

Interview coaching and practice is highly recommended. If there is an actual job interview coming up, then the time is ripe to partake in a video recorded practice interview. The interviewer could ask questions based on the job you are applying for.

To prepare for a real job interview:

- bring your career portfolio,
- dress appropriately,
- occasional smiling, humor and politeness is good,
- make certain you know the location and arrive 15 minutes early in case there is paperwork to fill out,
- use a firm handshake,
- maintain eye contact,
- wait on the interviewer to initiate the conversation as the interview progresses,
- breathe fully,
- actively listen to questions and answer with integrity, and
- try not to hurry your answers.
- Phew!

Make a checklist of the above pointers and after a few interviews it will flow naturally.

As the interview is wrapping up, you will be asked if you have any questions. These would be prepared beforehand as part of your preparation. This is another aspect of interviewing that a career advisor and/or coach could help with.

Be alert for when the interview is over, politely thank all in attendance by their first name preferably, shake hands and head out.

After the interview and before forgetting, write down any impressions and what you did well or could have done differently. Did you overlook sharing certain aspects such as relevant skills or experience? Did you feel comfortable with the interviewers, were they organized?

Shortly afterwards, send a concise thank you letter and include any highlights that came out of the interview such as your insight into a business problem that exists in their company.

If you're not hired, then the active targeted job search process is repeated again and you move forward with this experience under your belt. The employer you interviewed could become part of your network if permission is obtained and this could be addressed in a further note, email or phone call after finding out you were unsuccessful in the interview.

All the hard work will pay off when a job offer comes, which it will, and the odds are greatly increased that by using this system it will be a job that meets your needs and expectations!

How do I respond to a job offer?

Other than a manic feeling of excitement and desire to sing, there are two choices: accept or decline it.

If the job offer is accepted, you need to commit and follow through by taking the job. Contact any other employer that is interested in you for a different job, and let them know you are no longer available. Speak with these employers directly by phone as opposed to voicemail to convey your decisions. This would be followed up by well written letters or emails; one that accepts the job offer and another to the employer who was considering you.

If you need to decline a job offer, do so politely and with the intent of keeping this employer as part of your network. Speak to the employer rep. by phone and advise you are not accepting the offer and if necessary, provide a simple and polite reason why. Follow this up with an email that is sincere and thankful for their time and the opportunity to meet with them.

Negotiating a job offer

Certain employers may ask you what you expect for a starting wage or salary during the job offer phase. Others will state what the job pays and you may want to negotiate. If one of these possibilities happens, I would research salary information sources to respond to this development. This does not occur frequently, but is an opportunity to get paid what you are worth.

In addition to conducting an active targeted job search and if you are in need of support, government employment programs are another resource to check out.

Employment Programs for Older Workers

You have gained a wealth of knowledge and experience over your lifetime. Employers are seeking skilled workers with experience to help bridge the gaps. The key is connecting your skills and experiences to options now and in the future. Making informed, intentional choices will help you take stock of where you are now, where you want to go, how you are going to get there, while ensuring your choices support your chosen lifestyle.

Manitoba Government Career web-site[39]

There are a variety of government employment programs and initiatives that support older workers.

Examples of programs for older workers in Canada are described next. Similar initiatives exist in the USA and will differ depending on the state or region. These programs can change names over time but the scope of services provided would be similar.

Available across Canada is the Targeted Initiative for Older Workers and: "the TIOW is a federal-provincial/territorial cost-shared initiative that provides employment assistance services and employability improvement activities (such as skills upgrading and work experience), to unemployed older workers aged 55 to 64 living in communities experiencing ongoing high unemployment and/or with a high reliance on an industry significantly affected by down-sizing or closure."[36]

It is interesting that the TIOW program lasts until a worker is 64 and: "in some circumstances, unemployed workers aged 50 to 64 or 65 and over may also participate."[37] This is a government employment program that is not strictly tied to the 65 year old mark. For unretired Boomers who need to work past 65, it is a positive example of being supported by government policy.

Offered in the province of British Columbia, The Job Options BC Older Worker pro-gram: "is an employment and skills training program, located in Greater Vancouver, Greater Victoria, Kelowna and Nanaimo, that can help unemployed British Columbians, who are not EI eligible and who are 55 years of age and over gain the skills, confidence and experience they need to find employment."[38]

Following job loss and/or during a job search our primary focus is on the occupational dimension.

During times like this, remember to take time out for pampering, socializing, fun and of course, prioritizing **THE 4 FOUNDATIONAL LIFESTYLE HABITS**.

Up to this point in this five-chapter series on the occupational dimension, the emphasis was on working full time as an employee, which is known as standard employment. There has been a shift towards non-standard employment in the labor market. Non-standard employment includes part-time, casual, contract and *self-employment*.

Part of the reason for this is due to employers cutting costs by reducing the hour's employees work and associated health care, pension benefits and long term employment.

Self-employment offers some advantages over working as an employee and is elaborated upon in the next chapter on **Be Your Own Boss.**

BE YOUR OWN BOSS

Chapter Seventeen

*Nothing is really work unless you would
rather be doing something else*
J.M. Barrie

Un-retired *Boomers have accumulated a* wealth of knowledge and experience by this stage of their careers that could be transferable to *Be Your Own Boss*. Self-employment isn't without hurdles, but also offers an attractive upside for the older worker.

Flexible Hours and Work Location

We spend a significant amount of our life working. For an employee who works Monday to Friday at 8 hours per day, and is entitled to 7 weeks of holidays, including statutory days off, he or she spends 45 weeks (minus sick or other time away) or 225 days per year performing their job. For many employees, this requires travelling to a specified location and with the exception of lunch and breaks, remaining at the worksite for the duration of the day.

A big selling point for self-employment is that it can allow for more opportunity to attend to non-work matters. This isn't only important to Boomers but appears that Gen Y workers also understand and value this.

PwC's NextGen: A global generational study (2013) on the attitudes of millennials and how they compare to other generations: "has found that in order to foster a greater sense of commitment among

Millennials (those born between 1980 and 1995 and currently under 33 years of age) it will be necessary to transform the core dynamics of the workplace."[1] The study found that work-life balance and flexibility was high on the list for Gen Y and: "Just as notable, however, are the widespread similarities between millennial employees and their non-Millennial counterparts, all of whom aspire to a *new workplace paradigm* that places a higher priority on work/life balance and workplace flexibility."[2] Please find the reference for this ground breaking and fascinating study in the chapter notes, to learn more about how Gen Y is shaping the labor market.

The new workplace paradigm mentioned in the paragraph above, functions best for employees who work with information and telecommute. What makes this possible is technology, whether in the form of a mobile phone, tablet, desktop or all of these. In my work, faxes sent show up in my email and can be accessed anywhere there is an internet signal and forwarded or saved like any electronic file! Many mobile phones are capable of receiving email for several addresses and also be used for social media accounts such as Facebook, LinkedIn, Twitter and so on, or browsing the internet. A website, virtual private network and whatever business software programs are required becomes the hub or virtual office. This type of system is used by entrepreneurs around the world, and possibly you, if *Be Your Own Boss* is a viable option.

For employees who are tied to their work location such as teachers, those in the trades, retail and others, flexibility initiatives like a compressed work week, flex days, and paid days off, all move in the direction of a structure that allows for more time to tend to non-work activities. This was also discussed in *Chapter 13 on Work Stressors and Mental Health*.

Many people have had the dream about being their own boss and doing something they are passionate about. Self-employment offers the potential to start a business that is aligned with our strengths, interests and aspirations. Completing a self-assessment as covered in Chapter 16 with a career planning objective of self-employment would be a great exercise to determine if this is a suitable path and if so, to research a business idea.

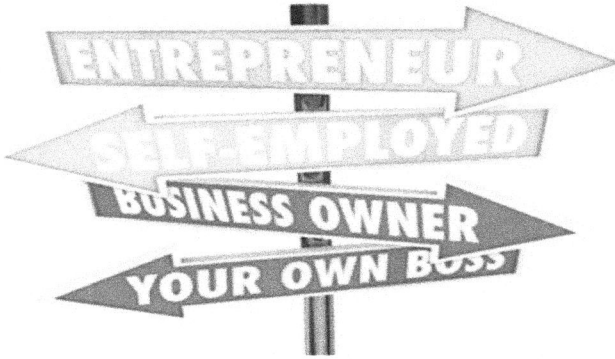

Additional upsides to self-employment includes more control over the following: taxation; income or profit; legacy; ageism; accommodation for disability and aging; conflicts with who you work with; and job loss, to name a few. It can also allow for a greater degree of meaning or purpose in our work.

As we live longer, there can be the need (unretired) to supplement retirement savings. A small business could be operated well into the mid to later stages of life to generate income.

In my duties as a career and/or rehabilitation counsellor, I have assisted individuals that chose the self-employment route as a career transition. Often their thinking at the outset was that a business could get up and off the ground with little planning. A small or large business venture requires a plan and this is elaborated on in an excerpt from the *Open Your New Business* website: "Technically, a business plan is a written statement of business goals, the reasons why they are attainable, and the plan for reaching those goals. Practically, if you want to start your own business, it is very important to go through the business plan process. It will help strengthen your new business idea, expose any weak links or show you how it just will not work. All of these things are very important to know "before" you start your business – not after you are committed."[3]

A business plan is a living document and for a small venture, can be completed fairly quickly and provides a baseline to build on.

If you qualify for a self-employment assistance program mentioned ahead, your business planning process is overseen by professionals.

Numbers of Boomers are checking out self-employment according to the TD Bank Group, who commissioned the Environics Research Group to conduct an online survey that found: "For Canadian Boomers, the road to retirement may include a stop as a small business owner. Whether starting freelance consulting work, buying a franchise or opening a specialty business, a recent TD Canada Trust survey found more than half of Boomers (54%) have started or considered starting a small business prior to retirement (15% and 39% respectively)."[4]

Becoming and succeeding as an entrepreneur requires assistance, and there is an abundance of free information and services available that support this. In Canada, there is a government program known as: "The Self-Employment Program which is funded by the Province of British Columbia and is designed for individuals who require ongoing financial and personal supports while developing and implementing their business plan. The program offers business management training and counseling for new entrepreneurs, and provides financial support for up to 48 weeks."[5]

In the United States, there is the Self-Employment Assistance program offered through the United States Department of Labor, Employment and Training Administration: "Self-Employment Assistance offers dislocated workers the opportunity for early re-employment. The program is designed to encourage and enable unemployed workers to create their own jobs by starting their own small businesses. Under these programs, States can pay a self-employed allowance, instead of regular unemployment insurance benefits, to help unemployed workers while they are establishing businesses and becoming self-employed. Participants receive weekly allowances while they are getting their businesses off the ground." [6]

The above government programs require that an applicant received or is receiving un/employment insurance benefits. These programs are available in most states and provinces and policies related to their eligibility will vary depending on your location.

A business venture could be started while employed, so you have a day job to fall back on. When the business is established and generating sufficient income the day job could be quit. Or working at both could continue, as long as needed or feasible to accelerate savings. I work full time, and for the last 2 years+ have spent a fair share of my spare time creating my platform as an authorpreneur on the side. I guess only time and planned effort will determine where this ends up!

There is limited security working as an employee and also no guarantee of success in developing any business. It should be a calculated risk and as Benjamin Franklin said: "Nothing ventured, nothing gained."

The use of a virtual office for a small business allows for low overhead and the ability to work location-free, anywhere there is an adequate internet connection. Living and working virtually in a country with a cheaper cost of living to leverage assets may not be for everybody, but is an option I'm looking at, as I write this guidebook.

Self-doubt is a normal reaction to issues like: what kind of business could I start; there is too much competition; am I suited to be a "Boomerpreneur" and so on. To address your concerns, begin by speaking to a community self-employment advisor and then decide where you go from there.

Your business should not own you, nor should it put your nest egg at risk, especially if it is a small egg! Some say it takes money to make money, or that you have to be comfortable losing money. I don't think these over used phrases are true beyond a shadow of doubt. Small business owners who are also un-retired Boomers need to manage financial risk and not jeopardize their assets. As a sole proprietor, business costs can entail borrowing money and turning to a commercial lender. An alternative source may be to look at forming innovative partnerships through a network such as RocketHub.

Rocket Hub is an online platform designed to raise money and is describes itself as: "Crowd funding is the act of many people contributing money to a project in exchange for a good or service, especially to expand and democratize opportunity: crowdfund the album; crowdfund the start-up; crowdfund the research; crowdfund the event."[7]

We can also learn from cultures such as those in India or China where extended families operate businesses collectively. By banding together to pool labor, financial and other resources to decrease overhead, all members young to old can be provided for.

It is now 17 chapters later after completing this one, on *Be Your Own Boss*. As I was doing the research for The Un-Retirement Guide™ I became aware (painfully at times) how much information has gone into these pages.

I hope that you enjoyed my creation and re-read chapters that you found helpful and are intellectually stimulated to keep learning!

A short chapter on Living Forward is next which considers the possibilities of the future. One lifetime and too many things to do and see!

LIVING FORWARD

When you stop growing you start dying
William S. Burroughs, Junkie

At this point you have read approximately 40,000+ words. It's small in comparison to many books, but I believe this guide is concise and packed with information. Thank you for coming along, in what for me was a challenging undertaking!

Did The Un-Retirement Guide™ answer the initial questions I asked in the introduction?

Answers usually generate more questions, digging and inquiring if you're like me.

I have given fair amount of thought on what to write in this **Living Forward** piece. Maybe an exam on the book content with prize money for the highest scores! I decided against this for a number of reasons, *like it might get expensive*!

So instead, I figured that just as I began the book with questions, I will end it with a few.

- How do you want to live/shape the years ahead?
- What dreams and goals do you want to fulfill?
- Do you want to live on purpose?
- Do you want to squeeze every drop out of the rest of your days?
- What is your personal definition of success?

These questions are certainly not unrealistic to ask of ourselves or accomplish.

I would expect no less from you...

The Un-Retirement Guide™ offers a holistic method to design our lifestyle as we live forward, through a Complete Life Wellness Plan™.

Like most worthwhile things in life, this requires some effort but is also fun and empowering!

There is valuable material waiting in the Appendices for you, *so let's head over there.*

APPENDICES

Welcome,

You might have completed Appendices A and B as you read through chapters 3 and 7 respectively, if not I recommend working through them first before moving onto complete life wellness planning.

Appendix A

Calculate the Cost of Your Standard of Living

Appendix B

Chronic Stress Symptom Inventory

My Gift to You: When you are ready, please go to this link/address for my website: *http://brianlukyn.com/companion-eBook/* to download at no charge, **A COMPLETE LIFE WELLNESS PLAN™** that covers all seven dimensions and much more.

If you have any questions or comments,
I would be glad to hear from you!

Reach me, through my website and/or email address below:

Brian.lukyn@gmail.com

www.brianlukyn.com

APPENDIX A

Calculate the Monthly Cost
of Your Standard of Living

Essential Living Expenses	Monthly Estimate	Notes	Non-Essential Expenses	Monthly Estimate	Notes
Housing, including property taxes if applicable			Travel and Vacations		
Utilities			Magazines and other subscriptions including pay per view		
Food and cleaning, bathroom supplies			Fitness memberships including the cost of golf, drop-in attendance at pools etc.		
Transportation, including fuel, maintenance			Eating out at restaurants		
Clothing, new linen as needed			Latest electronics		
Health expenses			Alcoholic beverages,		

(prescriptions, eye wear...)			tobacco		
Other expenses			Other expenses		
Monthly **Subtotal A** $_____			**Monthly** **Subtotal B** $_____	**Add the two monthly subtotals together** **(A +B)**	**Monthly cost of your standard of living** $____ **(A +B)**

APPENDIX B

Chronic Stress Symptom Inventory

I am not a medical practitioner and present the following information as such. If you have health concerns, please see your family doctor first to discuss them.

Potential symptoms of a chronic stress response are listed under the appropriate wellness dimensions below. Check the appropriate box below and add up how many of these symptoms you have experienced at the end of the inventory.

		✓ In the last three months, I have experienced these symptoms....		
DIMENSION	**OFTEN**	**SOME-TIMES**	**A FEW TIMES**	**NEVER**
INTELLECTUAL				
Loss of concentration				
Forgetfulness				
Lack of clarity in perception				
Memory difficulties				
EMOTIONAL/MENTAL				
Anxiety				
Moodiness				
Irritability/Short Temper				
Depression				

DIMENSION	OFTEN	SOME-TIMES	A FEW TIMES	NEVER
Anger				
Decreased sense of humour				
Abrasiveness				
Cry easily				
Apathy/lack of interest				
Negative self-talk				
Confusion				
Feeling overwhelmed				
SOCIAL				
Detached from others				
Intolerance				
Resentment				
Loneliness				
Lack of intimacy				
Hostility				
Distrust of others				
Nagging				
SPIRITUAL				
Loss of faith				
Loss of purpose or meaning				
Emptiness				
PHYSICAL				
Fatigue				
Cold hands or sweaty Palms				

DIMENSION	OFTEN	SOME-TIMES	A FEW TIMES	NEVER
Headaches				
Rapid heartbeat, chest pain				
Breathing difficulties				
Dizziness				
Loss of sex drive				
Insomnia or too much sleep				
Nausea				
Indigestion				
Diarrhea or constipation				
Nausea				
Indigestion				
Back pain				
Aches and pains				
Frequent cold				
NUMBER OF CHECKMARKS				
SCORE – Multiply the number of checkmarks in the three columns by the following:	____ x 3 = ————	____ x 2 = ————	____ x 1 = ————	

TOTAL SCORE- calculate the scores from each column. If you score mostly in the OFTEN column and or SOMETIMES columns, you may be experiencing the effects of a chronic stress response.

Additionally, the next section, is a further indication we are behaving in unhealthy ways to cope.

Indicators of Stress related Behaviours

The signs and symptoms listed in the above dimensions can produce changes in our behaviour such as:

- substance misuse and addiction, includes smoking

- excess sleeping or insomnia

- angry outbursts for what others perceive as not required

- no appetite or eating in excess

- playing video games or watching TV for hours on end

- being busy all the time

- excess caffeine intake

- procrastination or ignoring responsibilities

- nervous habits like foot tapping, nail biting or pacing

- self-destructive behaviour such as dangerous driving

Are you chronically stressed?

If your scores are high on the *Chronic Stress Symptom Inventory* (**Appendix B***)* and there are changes in behavior such as those listed above, a chronic stress response may be occurring. If you are concerned, discuss your situation with a physician, she/he will determine if any medical investigation and/or treatment is necessary. Once it is confirmed there is no major threat to your health (untreated high blood pressure, addiction, irregular heart rhythm, etc.), a plan to manage and minimize your stress load (chapter 7) could be initiated.

For best results, a wellness team would be put together that could include but not limited to your family physician and/or health nurse, wellness coach and of course, family and friends. Stress management would become an important goal in the emotional/mental dimension of your **COMPLETE LIFE WELLNESS PLAN™**.

Chapter Notes

CHAPTER ONE: WHEN CAN YOU RETIRE? I CAN'T YET

1. **Sun Life Canadian Unretirement Index**, 2013 Canadian Unretirement Index Report
   Retrieved from:
   http://www.sunlife.ca/Canada/sunlifeCA?vgnLocale=en_CA

2. **Labor Force Participation and Work Status of People 65 Years and Older**
   American Community Survey Briefs
   By Braedyn Kromer and David Howard Issued January 2013
   ACSBR/11-09 U.S. Department of Commerce Economics and Statistics Administration
   U.S. CENSUS BUREAU   census.gov

3. **National Seniors Council**
   www.seniorscouncil.gc.ca
   Older Workers At Risk of Withdrawing from the Labour Force or Becoming Unemployed: Employers' views on how to retain and attract older workers
   Retrieved from:
   http://www.seniorscouncil.gc.ca/eng/research_publications/older_workers/page05.shtml

4. **10 Reasons to Avoid Retirement**
   Retirement can have a negative impact on your finances, health and even your marriage.
   By Emily Brandon
   July 22, 2013

Retrieved from:
http://money.usnews.com/money/retirement/articles/2013/
07/22/10-reasons-to-avoid-retirement

CHAPTER TWO: FASCINATING FACTS ABOUT RETIREMENT, OR THE LACK THEREOF

1. **Encyclopedia of Death and Dying**
   Death and Dying » Ke-Ma » Life Expectancy
   Trends in Life Expectancy at Birth in Developed Countries
   Retrieved from:
   http://www.deathreference.com/Ke-Ma/Life-
   Expectancy.html#ixzz3OrDRwJWt
   *** The following source was included in the quotation:
   Yaukey, David, and Douglas L. Anderton. Demography: The
   Study of Human Population. Prospect Heights, IL: Waveland,
   2001.

2. Chapter 12, **"Work and Retirement," of Aging in Contemp-
   orary Canada** by Neena Chappell,
   Ellen Gee, Lynn McDonald and Michael Stones (Toronto:
   Prentice Hall, 2003).

3. *Schulz, J. H. **The Economics of Aging**, 4th ed. Dover, Mass.:
   Auburn House Publishing, 1988.

4. **The Mandatory Retirement Report in Brief**
   Mandatory Retirement
   A Violation of the Rights of Older Workers
   Submitted by
   CARP, Canada's Association for the Fifty-Plus July 2008

5. CARP, 2012
   **Mandatory Retirement – not dead yet: One Step Forward,
   Two Steps Backward**

Retrieved from:
http://www.carp.ca/2012/12/20/mandatory-retirement-not-dead-yet-one-step-forward-two-steps-backward/
Raymond D. Hall, is lead counsel for the Vilven-Kelly pilots' case and founder of FlyPast60 December 20, 2012

6. **Extending Work Life by Brian Alger**
   Retrieved from: http://exploring-life.ca/contact

7. Calgary & Area
   Labour Market Report
   Retirements and Mature Worker Retention Practices
   Results from the 2012 Employer Survey

8. **REINVENTING RETIREMENT – THE BOOMERS ARE NOT ALL RETIRING "ON SCHEDULE"**
   POSTED ON NOVEMBER 9, 2012
   Retrieved from:
   http://www.zoomermedia.ca/advertise/zoomer-u/reinventing-retirement-the-boomers-are-not-all-retiring-on-schedule

9. Kimberly Foss (2013)
   Wealthy by Design: A 5-Step Plan for Financial Security
   Retrieved from:
   http://money.usnews.com/money/retirement/articles/2013/07/22/10-reasons-to-avoid-retirement

10. **Health and Retirement: Planning for the Great Unknown 2014**
    A Merrill Lynch Retirement Study, conducted in partnership with *Age Wave-Retrieved from:
    https://www.wealthmanagement.ml.com/publish/content/application/pdf/GWMOL/MLWM_Health-and-Retirement-2014.pdf

11. **10 Reasons to Avoid Retirement**
Retirement can have a negative impact on your finances, health and even your marriage.
By Emily Brandon
July 22, 2013
Retrieved from:
http://money.usnews.com/money/retirement/articles/2013/07/22/10-reasons-to-avoid-retirement

CHAPTER THREE: WHAT STANDARD OF LIVING DO YOU WANT/DREAM OF?

1. **Beat the Retirement Blues with a One-Two Punch**
Retrieved from:
http://www.millersmoney.com/money-weekly/beat-the-retirement-blues-with-a-one-two-punch
2. Brickman & Campbell (1971). **Hedonic relativism and planning the good society**. New York: Academic Press. pp. 287–302.
3. **Poverty**
Retrieved from:
http://www.investopedia.com/terms/p/poverty.asp
4. **Low income cut-offs**
Statistics Canada, Government Canada
Retrieved from:
http://www.statcan.gc.ca/pub/75f0002m/2012002/lico-sfr-eng.htm
5. **Cost of Living**
Retrieved from:
http://www.investopedia.com/terms/c/cost-of-living

6. **Quality of Life Project**
    Chapter Eight, page 158
    Economic standard of living
    Quality of Life in Twelve of New Zealand's Cities (2007)
    Retrieved from:
    http://www.qualityoflifeproject.govt.nz/pdfs/2007/
    Quality_of_Life_2007_Standard.pdf

7. Employment and Social Development Canada
    Indicators of Well-being in Canada,
    Financial Security - Net Worth (Wealth)
    Retrieved from:
    http://www4.hrsdc.gc.ca/.3ndic.1t.4r@-eng.jsp?iid=84

8. Industry Fund Services
    How much income will I need?
    Retrieved from:
    http://www.ifs.net.au/retirement/planning-for-
    retirement/how-much-income-will-i-need/

9. Employment and Social Development Canada **Indicators of**
    Well-being in Canada
    Housing-Overview
    Human Resources and Skills Development Canada
    Retrieved from:
    http://www4.hrsdc.gc.ca/d.4m.1.3n@-eng.jsp?did=7

CHAPTER FOUR: BEHIND THE SCENES WITH HEALTH AND WELLNESS

1. **Older Workers At Risk of Withdrawing from the Labour**
    Force or Becoming Unemployed:
    Employers' views on how to retain and attract older
    workers
    March 2013. ISSD-124-03-13E
    THE NATIONAL SENIORS COUNCIL

http://www.seniorscouncil.gc.ca/eng/research_publications/older_workers/older_workers.pdf

2. **Genes, Behavior, and the Social Environment: Moving Beyond the Nature/Nurture Debate**
   Retrieved from:
   http://www.ncbi.nlm.nih.gov/books/NBK19932/
   Copyright © 2006, National Academy of Sciences.
   Bookshelf ID: NBK19932

3. Dr. Mike de Jong
   Neurotherapy and Neurofeedback ADHD Anxiety, Depression, OCD, Stress
   How Does Stress Affect Us?
   By AMERICAN PSYCHOLOGICAL ASSOCIATION
   Association, A. (2007). How Does Stress Affect Us? Psych Central. Retrieved on November 2, 2014, from:
   http://psychcentral.com/lib/how-does-stress-affect-us/0001130

4. **Understanding Wellness**
   Chapter 1 Page number 4
   A Wellness Way of Life, 9/edition
   Gwen Robbins, Ball State University
   Debbie Powers, Ball State University
   Sharon Burgess, Ball State University
   ISBN: 0073523836
   Copyright year: 2011

5. IBID to 4. Chapter 1, Page 4

6. Centers for Disease Control and Prevention
   Four Specific Health Behaviors Contribute to a Longer Life
   Ford ES, Zhao G, Tsai J, Li C. Low-risk lifestyle behaviors and all-cause mortality: Findings from the National Health and Nutrition Examination Survey III Mortality Study. American Journal of Public Health., published online ahead of print August 18, 2011.

Page last reviewed: August 15, 2011
Page last updated: August 31, 2011
Content source: Office of the Associate Director for Communication, Digital Media Branch, Division of Public Affairs

7. McGinnis, J. M., American Journal of Health Promotion 18 (Nov./Dec. 2003): 146–150

8. WebMD
    50+: Live Better, Longer
    Genes vs. Lifestyle: What Matters Most for Health?
    By Peter Jaret   WebMD Feature Reviewed by David T. Derrer, MD
    Retrieved from:
    http://www.webmd.com/healthy-aging/guide/genes-or-lifestyle

9. IBID to 4. (Chapter 1, page 2)

10. Spring 2011
    Lifescapes, Embracing Life
    PUBLISHED FOR FRIENDS & SUPPORTERS
    OF THE SIMPSON SENIOR SERVICES
    FAMILY OF COMMUNITIES.
    Retrieved from:
    http://www.simpsonsenior.org/wp-content/uploads/2012/02/LifeScapes3.8.11.pdf

11. Wellness Proposals Definitions of Wellness   **What is Wellness**
    http://wellnessproposals.com/wellness-articles/definition-of-wellness

12. Wikipedia
    Medical model
    Retrieved from:
    http://en.wikipedia.org/wiki/Medical_model

13. Preamble to the Constitution of the World Health Organization as adopted by the International Health Conference, New York, 19 June - 22 July 1946 (it entered into force on 7 April 1948)

14. IBID to 4—found on (Chapter 1, page 7)

15. The Wellness Workbook, 3rd ed:
    How to Achieve Enduring Health and Vitality – Apr 1 2004
    by John W. Travis (Author), Regina Sara Ryan (Author)

16. uOttawa   Society, the Individual and Medicine
    Definitions of Health
    Core Knowledge:
    Retrieved from:
    http://www.med.uottawa.ca/sim/data/Health_Definitions_e.htm
    The information on this site was assembled by Ian McDowell, Dep't of Epidemiology and Community Medicine, University of Ottawa,
    451 Smyth Road, Ottawa, Ontario, Canada, K1H 8M5

17. The National Wellness Institute
    About Wellness
    Applying Wellness
    Retrieved from:
    http://www.nationalwellness.org/?page=AboutWellnesS

CHAPTER FIVE: DESIGNING A WELLNESS LIFESTYLE

1. Wikipedia
   Positive Psychology
   Retrieved from:
   http://en.wikipedia.org/wiki/Positive_psychology
   ** Note: the last chapter is titled "Toward a Positive Psychology".

2. **Well-being, Wellness and Basic Human Needs in Home Economics**
McGregor Monograph Series No. 201003
October 18, 2010
Sue L. T. McGregor PhD Professor
Docent in Home Economics University of Helsinki
Doctoral Program Coordinator, Faculty of Education
Mount Saint Vincent University
Halifax NS B3M2J6
Retrieved from: http://www.consultmcgregor.com

CHAPTER SIX: LET'S GET PHYSICAL

1. Alliance for Aging Research
Adding Luster to Your Golden Years
Type: Feature Article
Date: Summer 2002
Related Topics; Health, Longevity, Quality of Care
Retrieved from:
http://archive-org.com/page/1244955/2013-01-28/http://www.agingresearch.org/content/article/detail/900

2. **The New Science of Aging: 4 Myths About How Your Body Ages**
By Gretchen Reynolds Published 04/12/2011
Retrieved from: http://www.oprah.com/health/Aging-Body-Changes-Aging-Myths

3. **Retirement Will Kill You.**
By Peter Orszag, Bloomberg, June 11, 2013.

4. AETNA
InteliHealth
The Trusted Source
The Importance of Nutrition

Retrieved from:
https://www.intelihealth.com/article/aetna-intelihealths-editorial-policy

5. Component of Statistics Canada Catalogue no. 82-003-X
    Health Reports
    Statistics Canada, Catalogue no. 82-003-XPE • Health Reports, Vol. 23, no. 4, December 2012
    The (NPHS
    Health behaviour changes after diagnosis of chronic illness among Canadians aged 50 or older.
    by Jason T. Newsom, Nathalie Huguet, Pamela L. Ramage-Morin, Michael J. McCarthy, Julie Bernier,
    Mark S. Kaplan and Bentson H. McFarland
    Released online November 21, 2012
    Retrieved from:
    http://www.statcan.gc.ca/pub/82-003-x/2012004/article/11740-eng.pdf

6. NCHPAD
    Building Healthy Inclusive Communities
    Food and Your Mood: Nutrition and Mental Health
    Retrieved from:
    http://www.nchpad.org/606/2558/Food~and~Your~Mood~~Nutrition~and~Mental~Health

7. National Sleep Foundation
    Sleep Hygiene
    Retrieved from: http://sleepfoundation.org/ask-the-expert/sleep-hygiene

8. Get Sleep
    Sleep and Health
    Retrieved from:
    http://healthysleep.med.harvard.edu/need-sleep/whats-in-it-for-you/health

9. Sleepless In America
    Why Is Sleep So Important?
    Depression and Bipolar Support Alliance Retrieved from:
    http://www.dbsalliance.org/site/PageServer?pagename=abo
    ut_sleep_why

10. Ibid to 7

11. Here to Help
    Mental health and Substance use information you can trust
    Wellness Module 6: Getting a Good Night's Sleep
    Retrieved from:
    http://www.heretohelp.bc.ca/wellness-module/wellness-
    module-6-getting-a-good-nights-sleep

12. Get Sleep
    Sleep and Health
    Retrieved from:
    http://healthysleep.med.harvard.edu/need-sleep/whats-
    in-it-for-you/health

13. Wellness Workbook: **How to Achieve Enduring Health and
    Vitality**
    By John W. Travis, Regina Sara Ryan
    3rd Edition 2004

14. Spinal Breath
    The Art of Conscious Breathing
    What is Conscious Breathing
    Retrieved from: http://spinalbreath.com/conscious-
    breathing/what-is-conscious-breathing/

15. Weil TM
    Andrew Weil MD
    Breathing, An Introduction
    Retrieved from:
    http://www.drweil.com/drw/u/ART00519/An-
    Introduction-to-Breathing.html

CHAPTER SEVEN: EMOTIONAL/MENTAL DIMENSION

1. Hales, D. 2005. An Invitation to Health, 11th ed. Belmont, CA: Thomson & Wadsworth.
    "An Invitation to Health for the Twenty-First Century"

2. **Inside Stressing Out: What works and what doesn't in the face of stress**
    March 24, 2014
    Retrieved from: http://www.heartmath.com/news/inside-stressing-out-what-works-and-what- doesnt-in-the-face-of-stress.html

3. Stress Symptoms, Signs, & Causes
    The Effects of Stress Overload and What You Can Do About It
    http://www.helpguide.org/mental/stress_signs.htm
    Authors: Melinda Smith, M.A., Robert Segal, M.A., and Jeanne Segal, Ph.D. Last updated: May 2014.
    http://www.helpguide.org/mental/stress_signs.htm
    '©Helpguide.org. All rights reserved. Helpguide.org is an ad-free non-profit resource for supporting better mental health and lifestyle choices for adults and children.'

4. Santa Clara University
    The Wellness Center
    Understanding Stress
    What is stress?
    Retrieved from:
    http://www.scu.edu/wellness/topics/understand.cfm

5. About Health
    Acute Stress
    Updated June 01, 2014.
    By Elizabeth Scott, M.S.
    Stress Management Expert

Retrieved from:
http://stress.about.com/od/stressmanagementglossary/g/accutestress.htm

6. Ibid to 3

7. Burnout Factor based on results from the 2011 Sun Life Canadian Health Index.
   SUN LIFE CANADIAN HEALTH INDEX TM
   The Burnout Factor. Understanding the far reaching impact of chronic stress on the health of employees and organizations Sun Life Canadian Health Index ᵀᴹ

8. Heart Math
   Inside Stressing Out: What works and what doesn't in the face of stress
   March 24, 2014
   Media contact: Gabriella "Gaby" Boehmer (831) 338-8710 or gboehmer@heartmath.com
   Retrieved from: http://www.heartmath.com/news/inside-stressing-out-what-works-and-what-doesnt-in-the-face-of-stress.html

   Note: This article may be reprinted in its entirety. Permission to reprint is contingent on the inclusion of the attribution statement "About HeartMath" found at the end of this article and inclusion of the embedded hyperlinks for online publications. The content herein may not be modified or altered without written permission from HeartMath.
   About HeartMath - The company's (www.heartmath.com) mission is to create a more coherent and heart-based world with less pain, suffering and more compassion, care and heart intelligence. For over two decades they have made significant contributions to the current knowledge about the vital role that the heart plays in mental health and physical wellness. HeartMath research studies demonstrate a critical link between emotions, heart function and cognitive performance and are published in numerous peer-reviewed

journals. Based on this research, the company provides unique services, products and technologies to improve well-being and reduce emotional stress. Their award-winning Inner Balance and emWave technologies have more than 300,000 users. Most recently, HeartMath released their free HeartCloudTM platform where customers can synch session data in one location, earn practice rewards and more. HeartCloud is the next step in building a community of connected hearts. HeartCloud is a valuable resource of anonymous HRV data that can be studied and used for larger implications of collective coherence on a global scale.

HeartCloudTM, Inner BalanceTM and emWave® are trademarks of Quantum Intech. HeartMath® is a trademark of the Institute of HeartMath. IPhone®, iPod and iPad® are trademarks of Apple

9. University of Twente
   Theory Clusters
   Transactional Model of Stress and Coping
   Retrieved from:
   http://www.utwente.nl/cw/theorieenoverzicht/theory%20clusters/health%20communication/transactional_model_of_stress_and_coping/
   Additional sources used for reference number 10:
   Antonovsky, A. & Kats, R. (1967). "The Life Crisis History as a Tool in Epidemiologic Research". Journal of Health and Social Behavior, 8, 15-20.
   Cohen, F. (1984). "Coping" In J.D. Matarazzo, S.M. Weiss, J.A. Herd, N.E. Miller & S.M. Weiss (eds.), Behavioral Health: A Handbook of Health Enhancement and Disease Prevention. New York: Wiley, 1984.
   Lazarus, R.S. & Cohen, J.B. (1977). "Environmental Stress". In I. Altman and J.F. Wohlwill (eds.), Human Behavior and Environment. (Vol 2) New York: Plenum.

10. Stress Management for Health Course
    Causes of Stress
    Retrieved from: http://stresscourse.tripod.com/id14.html

11. Psychology Today
    PSYCH BASICS
    Resilience
    (failure, rejection, grit)
    All About Resilience
    Retrieved from:
    http://www.psychologytoday.com/basics/resilience

12. Ibid to 9

CHAPTER EIGHT: INTELLECTUAL DIMENSION

1. MedRounds
   The Encyclopedia of Aging & The Elderly
   By Hampton Roy, M.D. & Charles Russell, PH.D
   SUNDAY, DECEMBER 11, 2005 achievements at an advanced
   age, ACTION, Active Corps of Executives
   Retrieved from:
   http://www.medrounds.org/encyclopedia-of-
   aging/2005/12/achievements-at-advanced-age-
   action.html

2. Lumosity
   About Lumosity
   Retrieved from: http://www.lumosity.com/about

3. Freiman, M., Brown, E. Special care units in nursing homes -
   selected characteristics, 1996. Rockville (MD): Agency for
   Health Care and Policy Research 1999. MEPS Research
   Findings   No.   6.   AHCPR   Pub.   No.   99-0017.

4. Alzheimer's Foundation of America
   About Dementia
   Retrieved from:
   http://www.alzfdn.org/AboutDementia/definition.html
   Reducing the risk of developing Dementia through our Lifestyle Habits

5. **Rising Tide: The Impact of Dementia on Canadian Society**
   ISBN 978-0-9733522-2-1
   ® 2010 Alzheimer Society of Canada
   Rising Tide: The Impact of Dementia on Canadian Society is a report based on a study conducted by RiskAnalytica. The Rising Tide project was made possible with contributions from the Canadian Institutes of Health Research, the Public Health Agency of Canada, Health Canada, Pfizer Canada and Rx&

6. 2015 Alzheimer Society of Canada
   About Dementia
   Dementia numbers in Canada
   Retrieved from:
   http://www.alzheimer.ca/en/About-dementia/What-is-dementia/Dementia-number

7. The importance of our sleeping is mentioned in chapter 5 where the Division of Sleep Medicine at Harvard Medical School
   Get Sleep
   Sleep and Health
   Retrieved from:
   http://healthysleep.med.harvard.edu/need-sleep/whats-in-it-for-you/health

8. IBID to 4
   Rising Tide: The Impact of Dementia on Canadian Society
   ISBN 978-0-9733522-2-1
   ® 2010 Alzheimer Society of Canada

CHAPTER NINE: SPIRITUAL DIMENSION

1. **Spirit**
   Retrieved from: http://en.wikipedia.org/wiki/Spirit

2. **Religion and Spirituality in the Elderly**
   Retrieved from:
   http://www.merckmanuals.com/professional/geriatrics/so
   cial issues in the elderly/religion and spirituality in th
   e elderly.html

3. **TAKING CHARGE OF YOUR HEALTH AND WELLBEING**
   Created by the Center for Spirituality & Healing and Charlson
   Meadows.
   What Is Spirituality?
   Retrieved from:
   http://www.takingcharge.csh.umn.edu/enhance-your-
   wellbeing/purpose/spirituality/what-spirituality
   A collaboration between University of Minnesota-Center for
   Spirituality & Healing and Charlson Meadows renewal center

4. **Spirituality and Aging**
   http://cas.umkc.edu/casww/sa/spirituality.htm

5. **Understanding Wellness**
   Chapter 1, page number 10
   A Wellness Way of Life, 9/edition
   Gwen Robbins, Ball State University
   Debbie Powers, Ball State University
   Sharon Burgess, Ball State University
   ISBN: 0073523836
   Copyright year: 2011

6. Mauk, K. (2006). Gerontological Nursing: Competencies for
   Care. Sudbury, MA. Jones & Bartlett Publishers.

7. Amy Banks , M.D., director of Advanced Training at the Jean
   Baker Miller Training Institute at the Wellesley Centers for
   Women ; instructor of Psychiatry at Harvard Medical School;
   co-editor of The Complete Guide to Mental Health for

Women; and author of Post-Traumatic Stress Disorder: Relationships and Brain Chemistry.
Copyright ©2015 Jean Baker Miller Training Institute, Wellesley Centers for Women, Wellesley College Humans are hardwired for connection? Neurobiology 101 for parents, educators, & the general public
September 15, 2010
Retrieved from: http://www.jbmti.org/Media-Coverage/humans-are-hardwired-for-connection-neurobiology-101-for-parents-educators-a-the-general-public

CHAPER TEN: SOCIAL DIMENSION

1. University of Cincinnati
   College of Nursing
   Center for Aging with Dignity
   Safe After 60
   Social Wellness
   An initiative of the College of Nursing at the University of Cincinnati, the Center collaborates with experts in a variety of fields (e.g. Criminal Justice, Medicine, Social Work)
   Retrieved from:
   http://nursing.uc.edu/centers/aging_with_dignity/exploring_aging/gero_gems/social_wellness.html

2. Read more at
   http://www.brainyquote.com/quotes/quotes/a/atulgawand527239.html#uAxUCJ5JpIvqBo1v.99

3. Daniel Goleman

From the prologue to Social Intelligence
Daniel Goleman, Ph.D., author of the New York Times bestseller
Emotional Intelligence and Social Intelligence: The New Science of Human Relationships.
Retrieved from:
http://www.danielgoleman.info/topics/social-intelligence/

4. Amy Banks , M.D., director of Advanced Training at the Jean Baker Miller Training Institute at the Wellesley Centers for Women ; instructor of Psychiatry at Harvard Medical School; co-editor of The Complete Guide to Mental Health for Women; and author of Post-Traumatic Stress Disorder: Relationships and Brain Chemistry.
Copyright ©2015 Jean Baker Miller Training Institute, Wellesley Centers for Women, Wellesley College Humans are hardwired for connection? Neurobiology 101 for parents, educators, & the general public
September 15, 2010
Retrieved from: http://www.jbmti.org/Media-Coverage/humans-are-hardwired-for-connection-neurobiology-101-for-parents-educators-a-the-general-public

5. Communication studies
The #1 Resource for the Communication Field
What is Communication? The Definition of Communication
Retrieved from:
http://www.communicationstudies.com/what-is-communication

6. BBC
Languages Other
Retrieved from:
http://www.bbc.co.uk/languages/guide/languages.shtml

7. **Hands On Research: The Science of Touch**

By Dacher Keltner | September 29, 2010 | 5 Comments
Dacher Keltner explains how compassion is literally at our
fingertips.
Retrieved from:
http://greatergood.berkeley.edu/article/item/hands_on_r
esearch

8. **Intimate relationship**
   Retrieved from:
   http://en.m.wikipedia.org/wiki/Intimate_relationship

9. ASK
   What are social needs?
   Retrieved from:
   http://www.ask.com/world-view/social-needs-
   8e3901f003c9203e#full-answer

10. Public Health Agency of Canada
    www.publichealth.gc.
    Underlying Premises and Evidence Table
    What Makes Canadians Healthy or Unhealthy?
    KEY DETERMINANT -- 2. Social Support Networks
    Retrieved from: http://www.phac-aspc.gc.ca/ph-
    sp/determinants/determinants-eng.php

CHAPTER ELEVEN: ENVIRONMENTAL DIMENSION

1. University of Illinois
   Wellness Centre
   Environmental Wellness
   Definition
   Retrieved from:
   http://www.campusrec.illinois.edu/wellnesscenter/dimen
   sions/environmental.html

CHAPTER TWELVE: OCCUPATIONAL DIMENSION

1. Rich Dad
   Financial education Blog
   The definition of wealth
   Robert Kiyosaki May 28, 2013
   Retrieved from: http://www.richdad.com/Resources/Rich-Dad-Financial-Education-Blog/May-2013/the-definition-of-wealth.aspx

CHAPTER 13: WORK LIFE STRESSORS

1. World Health Organization
   Mental health: strengthening our response
   Fact sheet N°220
   Updated August 2014
   Retrieved from:
   http://www.who.int/mediacentre/factsheets/fs220/en/

2. The American Institute of Stress
   Workplace Stress
   Retrieved from: http://www.stress.org/workplace-stress/

3. Press Release June 19, 2013
   Job insecurity and difficulties balancing work and family are key components of mental health issues in the workplace.
   Results of an extensive study of worker's mental health.
   These findings, disclosed today, are the results of the largest research study ever conducted on the subject in Canada. The study was undertaken by researchers at the Université de Montréal, Concordia University and Université Laval with the support of Standard Life.
   Retrieved from:
   http://www.standardlife.ca/en/media/press/news/2013/june19_2013.html

4. The British Columbia, Ministry of Health
   Healthy Living
   Organizational Wellness
   Retrieved from:
   http://www.health.gov.bc.ca/environments/workplace/or
   gwellness.html

5. HBR Blog Network (Harvard Business Review)
   Work-Life "Balance" Isn't the Point
   by Christine M. Riordan Harvard Business Review   Her
   research focuses on labor-force diversity issues, leadership
   effectiveness, and career success.
   Retrieved from: https://hbr.org/2013/06/work-life-balance-
   isnt-the-poi/

6. Shepell•fgi
   Work/Life Balance - For the Good of Your Health
   Retrieved from: http://www.shepellfgi.com

7. The Balance Sheet
   Health, Balance and Wellbeing May 29 2012
   Mental Health in the Workplace
   PPC Canada is a long established (since 1977) Employee and
   Family Wellness Program provider with a reputation for
   quality with integrity. A pioneer in the field of Employee and
   Family Assistance (EFAP), we currently provide responsive
   and individualized services to more than 350 organizations
   across Canada.
   Retrieved from:
   http://www.ca.ppcworldwide.com/newsletters/newsletter
   s/pdf3/the%20Balance%20Sheet%20-
   %20May%202012.pdf

CHAPTER 14: HITTING IT HEAD-ON – DEALING WITH AGEISM

1. **Policy on discrimination against older people because of age**
   Ontario Human Rights Commission
   Employment
   Retrieved from: http://www.ohrc.on.ca/en/policy-discrimination-against-older-people-because-age/2-%E2%80%9Cage%E2%80%9D-%E2%80%9Colder%E2%80%9D-person-and-human-rights-concepts

2. Fight Age Discrimination, Stay Positive
   By Jen Laskey
   Dealing with age discrimination can be emotionally difficult, but you might be surprised to learn what older Americans are doing to empower themselves—and others.
   Retrieved from:
   http://www.everydayhealth.com/longevity/emotional-wellness/fighting-age-discrimination.aspx

3. About Careers
   Discrimination Laws
   Guide to Employment Discrimination Laws and Issues
   By Alison Doyle
   Retrieved from:
   http://jobsearch.about.com/od/hiringdiscrimination/tp/employment-discrimination.htm

4. Career Path 360
    Every topic Every angle
    Employment Law
    Ageism, Age Discrimination, Older Workers not Retiring Working after Retirement.
    By: Kacey Stapleton
    Published: February 4, 2009
    Retrieved from:
    http://www.careerpath360.com/index.php/ageism-age-discrimination-eeoc-older-workers-not-retiring-working-after-retirement-17312/

5. Older Adults-Aging in Canada
    Friday, 7 December 2012
    Older Adults in the Canadian Workforce: EAPs and Training from a Liberal Perspective
    Retrieved from:
    http://olderadultsswrk1006.blogspot.ca/2012/12/older-adults-in-canadian-workforce-eaps.html

6. Aging Workers
    Canadian Centre for Occupational Health and Safety
    Are training requirements different for older workers?
    Retrieved from:
    http://www.ccohs.ca/oshanswers/psychosocial/aging_workers.html

7. Career Path 360
    Every topic Every angle
    Employment Law
    Ageism, Age Discrimination, Older Workers not Retiring Working after Retirement.
    By: Kacey Stapleton
    Published: February 4, 2009
    Retrieved from:
    http://www.careerpath360.com/index.php/ageism-age-discrimination-eeoc-older-workers-not-retiring-working-after-retirement-17312/

8. US Administration on Aging c/o
    Diversity Employment Services
    50-plus and Looking for Work?
    Posted on December 12, 2013 By adminadult, Who needs a job?
    Employment Service Finds Senior Jobs
    By Sharon O'Brien
    Retrieved from:
    http://www.diversityemploymentservices.com/50-plus-and-looking-for-work/

9. Ministry of Business, Innovation and Employment New Zealand
    Department of Labour
    Hikina Whakatutuki Labour Information
    Home > Research Centre > Labour Market and Skills > Workforce2020 Myth busting factsheet
    Too old for the job? No Way!
    Retrieved from:
    http://www.dol.govt.nz/services/LMI/workforce2020/myths/older-workers.asp

CHAPTER 15: CAREER MANAGEMENT FOR EMPLOYEES

1. Businessdictionary.com
   Career Management
   Retrieved from:
   http://www.businessdictionary.com/definition/career-management.html#ixzz3g0CPm8UW

2. What is a Career? By Dawn Rosenberg McKay Career Planning Expert
   About Careers
   Retrieved from:
   http://careerplanning.about.com/od/careerchoicechan/f/career-faq.htm

3. **The Career - Life - Work Series, Planning Your Career Workbook**
   Retrieved from:
   http://www.nwt.literacy.ca/resources/adultlit/career_life_work/planning_your_career_workbook.pdf

   The NWT Literacy Council gratefully acknowledges the financial assistance for this project from the Department of Education, Culture and Employment, Government of the Northwest Territories.

4. Introduction to New Paradigm for Life planning
   Tuesday, May 31, 2011
   Towards Integrative Life Planning - Introduction to ILP Part 1 of 8
   Retrieved from:
   http://balancedlifesa.blogspot.ca/2011/05/towards-integrative-life-planning-part.html

5. ERIC Identifier: ED482538
    Publication Date: 2003
    Author: Imel, Susan
    Source: ERIC Clearinghouse on Adult Career and Vocational Education
    Career Development of Older Adults. ERIC Digest.
    Retrieved from: http://www.ericdigests.org/2005-1/older.htm
    The following sources of information were used by Susan Imel (2003) (4
    **Hall, D. T. Careers in and out of Organizations. Thousand Oaks, CA: Sage, 2002.
    **Riverin-Simard, D. "Career Development in a Changing Context of the Second Part of Working Life." In The Future of Career, edited by A. Collin and R. A. Young. Cambridge, UK: Cambridge University Press, 2000.
    ** Hall, D. T. Careers in and out of Organizations. Thousand Oaks, CA: Sage, 2002.

6. Career Continuum
    Your Career Life is a Journey!
    Remaining relevant at the speed of light (2009)
    Retrieved from:
    http://careercontinuum.wordpress.com/tag/social-networking/

7. Holmes and Rahe stress scale
    Holmes TH, Rahe RH (1967). "**The Social Readjustment Rating Scale**". J Psychosom Res 11
    Retrieved from:
    http://en.m.wikipedia.org/wiki/Holmes_and_Rahe_stress_scale

CHAPTER 16: CAREER PLANNING AND CONDUCTING A TARGETED JOB SEARCH

1. Business Dictionary.com
   Read more:
   http://www.businessdictionary.com/definition/career-planning.html#ixzz3YoXRJ1Irg

2. Retrieved from: https://www.workbc.ca/Job-Seekers/Build-Your-Career/Planning-Your-Career/Starting-and-Planning-Your-Career/Self-assessment.aspx#sthash.M2YKk8FM.dpuf

3. Skills
   Retrieved from: http://www.merriam-webster.com/dictionary/skill

4. Soft Skills – Ask a Wharton MBA
   SOFT SKILLS DEFINITION: WHAT ARE SOFT SKILLS?
   Retrieved from:
   https://bemycareercoach.com/softskills/what-are-soft-skills

5. Hard Skills vs. Soft Skills
   The Difference Between Hard Skills and Soft Skills
   By Alison Doyle
   Job Searching Expert
   Retrieved from:
   http://jobsearch.about.com/od/skills/qt/hard-soft-skills.htm

6. Quintessential Careers
   Empowering Job Seekers since 1996
   What Do Employers Really Want? Top Skills and Values Employers Seek from Job-Seekers
   Retrieved from:
   http://www.quintcareers.com/job_skills_values.html

7. Laurier Career Development Center
   Marketing your Transferable Skills
   Retrieved from:
   https://navigator.wlu.ca/content/documents/fileItemCont
   roller/GRAD%20Marketing%20Your%20Transferable%20Sk
   ills%202011-12.pdf

8. Job Interview Tools
   Career Aptitude Test and Job Aptitude Tests
   by Don Georgevich
   Retrieved from:
   http://www.jobinterviewtools.com/career-aptitude-test.htm

9. Stanford University
   Career Development Center
   Self-Assessments
   Retrieved from:
   https://studentaffairs.stanford.edu/cdc/identify/self-
   assessments

10. Job-Interview-Site.com
    Job Interview & Career Guide
    **Are you Thinking of a Career Change? Discover Your
    Transferable Skills**
    http://www.job-interview-site.com/transferable-skills-list-of-
    transferable-skills-examples-for-career-changers.html

11. Transferable Skills Alone Won't win that Job
    **How to sell transferable skills to new employers and land a
    job in a new industry.**
    By Joe Turner
    Retrieved from: http://info.theladders.com/career-
    advice/transferable-skills-alone-wont-win-job

12. SaskNetWork
    Discover how far you can go in Saskatchewan
    Values, Skills and Personal Style
    Retrieved from:
    http://www.sasknetwork.ca/html/JobSeekers/careerplann
    ing/yourvalues.htm

13. Psychometrics   Building Better Organizations Through
    People
    Myers-Briggs logo
    MYERS-BRIGGS TYPE INDICATOR ® (MBTI ®)
    MEASURE PERSONALITY TYPE
    Retrieved from:
    http://www.psychometrics.com/default.aspx?

14. Johnson O'Connor Research Foundation
    Aptitude testing for career and educational guidance
    Retrieved from:
    http://www.jocrf.org/about_aptitudes/index.html

15. About careers
    Self-Assessment
    An Overview
    By Dawn Rosenberg McKay
    Career Planning Expert
    Retrieved from:
    http://careerplanning.about.com/cs/aboutassessment/a/ass
    ess_overview.htm

16. Career Thought Leaders
    Overcoming Any Employment Barrier, Part 2
    Step 1: Identify the barrier
    By Elisabeth H. Sanders-Park, CWDP, JCTC
    This article appeared originally in the Career Planning & Adult Development Network Newsletter.
    Retrieved from:
    http://www.careerthoughtleaders.com/library/tough-career-transitions/overcoming-any-employment-barrier-part-2/

17. Iseek
    Minnesota's career, education and job resource.
    Barriers to Employment
    A physical condition or personal situation can make it hard to find or keep a job.
    Retrieved from:
    https://www.iseek.org/jobs/barriers-employment.html

18. English Dictionary
    Pioneers in dictionary publishing since 1819
    Retrieved from:
    http://www.collinsdictionary.com/dictionary/english/labour-market

19. **What is labour market information? Do I need it?**
    Retrieved from:
    http://settlement.org/ontario/employment/find-a-job/labour-market-information/what-is-labour-market-information-do-i-need-it/

20. Human Resource Development Canada
    Occupational Outlook
    Planning and AnalysisPA-BCYT-07-96E
    Choosing a Career   1996 Edition

21. **The National Occupational Classification and the Career Handbook**
Retrieved from:
http://www30.hrsdc.gc.ca/noc/English/CH/2001/Introduct ionNOCandCH.aspx

22. **Job Titles vs. Occupation: What Job Seekers Need to Know**
by Mary Marino on SEPTEMBER 21, 2011 in JOB SEARCH
Retrieved from:
http://www.employmentpipeline.com/blog/?s=job+titles&su bmit.x=0&submit.y=0

23. **Job Titles vs. Occupation: What Job Seekers Need to Know**
by Mary Marino on SEPTEMBER 21, 2011 in JOB SEARCH
Retrieved from:
http://www.employmentpipeline.com/blog/?s=job+titles&su bmit.x=0&submit.y=0

24. **Welcome to the National Occupational Classification 2011**
Retrieved from:
http://www5.hrsdc.gc.ca/NOC/English/NOC/2011/AboutNO C.aspx

25. **Welcome to the Career Handbook**
Retrieved from:
http://www5.hrsdc.gc.ca/NOC/English/CH/2001/Welcome.as px23

26. **Overview of BLS Statistics by Occupation** (www.bls.gov)
2010 SOC User Guide FAQs and Acknowledgements, 2010 SOC
U.S. Bureau of Labor Statistics
On behalf of the Standard Occupational Classification Policy Committee (SOCPC)
Retrieved from:
www.bls.gov21

27. Jobseeker or Worker
    Explore Careers
    Occupational Outlook Handbook
    Retrieved from:
    http://www.bls.gov/audience/jobseekers.htm

28. JOB SEARCH TIPS & HELPTRUSTED RESOURCES FOR YOUR
    FLEXIBLE JOB SEARCH
    TELECOMMUTING FREELANCE PART-TIME FLEXIBLE
    Retrieved from:
    http://www.flexjobs.com/blog/post/questions-ask-
    informational-interview/
    22 Sep, 2014
    Questions to Ask in an Informational Interview
    Jessica Howington
    FlexJobs Online Job Researcher and Writing Team Lead

29. Indiana University Bloomington
    The Media School Journalism
    Informational Interviews
    Retrieved from:
    http://journalism.indiana.edu/media-
    careers/resources/information-interviews/

30. Job Star Central
    Hidden Job Market - What is it?
    Retrieved from:
    http://jobstar.org/hidden/hidden.php

31. Forbes
    The Muse Contributor
    1/29/2012 @ 12:07PM 145,106 views
    Is a Skills-Based Resume Right for You?
    Retrieved from:
    http://www.forbes.com/sites/dailymuse/2012/01/29/is-a-
    skills-based-resume-right-for-you/1

32. Laurier Career Development Center
Marketing your Transferable Skills
Retrieved from:
https://navigator.wlu.ca/content/documents/fileItemCont
roller/GRAD%20Marketing%20Your%20Transferable%20Sk
ills%202011-12.pdf

33. **Cover Letters Build the Case for Workers Over 50**
By John Rossheim, Monster Senior Contributing Writer
Retrieved from: http://career-
advice.monster.com/resumes-cover-letters/cover-letter-
tips/cover-letters-for-50-plus-workers/article.aspx

34. Quintessential Careers
Empowering Job Seekers since 1996
**What Do Employers Really Want? Top Skills and Values
Employers Seek from Job-Seekers**
Retrieved from:
http://www.quintcareers.com/job_skills_values.html

35. Job Hunt
Your Search for a Smarter Job Search
Phyllis Mufson
Networking: the Boomer Job Search Advantage
Retrieved from:
http://www.job-hunt.org/boomer-job-search/boomer-job-
search-advantage.shtml

36. Canada Economic Action Plan
Jobs and Opportunities
Targeted Initiative for Older Workers
http://actionplan.gc.ca/en/initiative/targeted-initiative-
older-workers
Funding: Employment Assistance for Older Workers
Retrieved from:
http://www.esdc.gc.ca/eng/jobs/training_agreements/old
er_workers/index.shtml

37. Canada Economic Action Plan
Jobs and Opportunities
Targeted Initiative for Older Workers
http://actionplan.gc.ca/en/initiative/targeted-initiative-older-workers
Funding: Employment Assistance for Older Workers
Retrieved from:
http://www.esdc.gc.ca/eng/jobs/training_agreements/older_workers/index.shtml

38. **B.C. Labour Market Programs   Job Options BC**
Retrieved from: http://www.workbc.ca/Job-Seekers/Build-Your-Career/Planning-Your-Career/Starting-and-Planning-Your-Career/BC-Employment-Programs.aspx

39. Manitoba.ca
Career Development
Older Worker
Retrieved from:
http://www.manitobacareerdevelopment.ca/CDi/older_worker_career_development.html

CHAPTER 17: BE YOUR OWN BOSS

1. PwC's NextGen:
A global generational study
Retrieved from: http://www.pwc.com/en_GX/gx/hr-management-services/pdf/pwc-nextgen-study-2013.pdf

2. PwC's NextGen:
A global generational study
Retrieved from: http://www.pwc.com/en_GX/gx/hr-management-services/pdf/pwc-nextgen-study-2013.pdf

3. Open Your New Business
Business Plan Guide
How to Write a Complete Business Plan
Retrieved from:
http://www.openmynewbusiness.com/business-plan-guide/

4. CNW, A PR Newswire Company
October 9, 2012 8:30 AM - Financial - Surveys - Financial Services
Canadian boomers catch entrepreneurial bug
TD Bank Group commissioned Environics Research Group to conduct an online omnibus survey of 1,000 Canadians 18 years of age or older, with 426 who are considered part of the Baby boomer generation (born 1946 and 1964). Results were collected between September 26 and 28, 2012. Retrieved from:
http://www.newswire.ca/en/story/1048979/canadian-boomers-catch-entrepreneurial-bug

5. Community Futures Boundary
Growing communities' one idea at a time.
About the Self-Employment Program What You Need To Know:
Retrieved from: http://www.boundarycf.com/self-employment/about-program

6. United States Department of Labor
UNITED STATES DEPARTMENT OF LABOR
Employment & Training Administration
Self-Employment Assistance
Retrieved from:
http://workforcesecurity.doleta.gov/unemploy/self.asp

7. RocketHub
   The world's crowdfunding machine
   Master the Basics
   What's Crowdfunding?
   Retrieved from:
   http://www.rockethub.com/education/basics

ADDITIONAL REFERENCES FOR CHAPTER 4:
BEHIND THE SCENES WITH HEALTH AND   WELLNESS

- **Healthy.net**
  Healthy People   Healthy Planet
  Seeking natural solutions for your health?
  ... more vitality ... enhanced wellbeing
  You're in the right place!
  Explore our health village, join our community begin your wellness journey.
  Retrieved from: http://www.healthy.net

- **WellPeople:** the whole person wellness solution
  Wellness training at the personal and coaching level
  Retrieved from: http://www.wellpeople.com/

- **The American Institute of Stress**
  "The mission of AIS is to improve the health of the community and the world by setting the standard of excellence of stress management in education, research, clinical care and the workplace. Diverse and inclusive, The American Institute of Stress educates medical practitioners, scientists, health care professionals and the public; conducts research; and provides information, training and techniques to prevent human illness related to stress."
  Retrieved from: http://www.stress.org/stress-effects/

- **Quantum Coaching Method**
  Personal coaching and various programs to train coaches
  Retrieved from;
  http://quantumcoachingmethod.com/about/marilena/

- **World Health Organization**   A wealth of global health
  Information.
  "Our primary role is to direct and coordinate international
  health within the United Nations' system.
  These are our main areas of work:
  Health systems
  Promoting health through the life-course
  Non-communicable diseases
  Communicable diseases
  Corporate services
  Preparedness, surveillance and response"
  Retrieved from: http://www.who.int/en/

- **National Wellness Institute**   a non-profit organization promoting wellness globally
  Provides certifications in wellness and continuing education
  "Founded in 1977, the National Wellness Institute, Inc. (NWI)
  was formed to realize the mission of providing health
  promotion and wellness professionals unparalleled resources
  and services that fuel professional and personal growth."
  Retrieved from: http://www.nationalwellness.org/

- Canadian Wellness
  "Canadian Wellness is a comprehensive directory of fitness,
  diet, health, nutrition and other wellness related profess-
  sionals and their services."
  Retrieved from: http://www.canadianwellness.com/

- **American Holistic Health Association**
  The free and impartial wellness resource.
  "Our sole purpose is to offer you impartial holistic health resources— both alternative and traditional —that help you become more active and confident in your health decisions."
  Retrieved from: http://ahha.org/wellness.asp

End of Chapter Notes

The COMPLETE LIFE WELLNESS PLAN™ (Gift Companion E-Book)

1. **Get Sleep**
   Sleep and Health
   Retrieved from:
   http://healthysleep.med.harvard.edu/need-sleep/whats-in-it-for-you/health

2. **Live Life Well, Achieve Health and Happiness**
   Lifestyle, Health and Wellness Concepts
   Intellectual Wellness Dimension
   Retrieved from: LiveLifeWell.com

3. UNC CHARLOTTE
   Your Health,
   Advisory Committee to the Chancellor for Employee Health and Wellness
   Occupational Dimension
   Retrieved from:
   http://yourhealth.uncc.edu/dimensions-wellness

IMAGES

The images in **The Un-Retirement Guide™** and Companion eBook are a combination of the author's, one image of the bull rider in chapter 13 by J.M. Lukyn and the remainder are sourced from Canstockphoto.com with permission.